Effects of

Yogic Practices

Among School Children

Sohail Mihani

CONTENTS

Page No.

LIST OF GRAPHS

Chapter I

INTRODUCTION

We are living in a world which is full of technologically produced information. Despite the availability of a number of means of pleasure and happiness in this ultra-scientific age, our lives are mired by a plethora of diseases of both sorts; old and new. Under such circumstances, our ancient Vedic culture of Yoga has become a panacea for all diseases. Not only India, but the whole of the world has recognized the power and importance of yoga. United Nations Organization, on witnessing the miraculous soothing and healing power of yogic activities, has decided to popularize India's ancient Vedic formula of Yoga by celebrating International Yoga Day every year on 21 June since 2015, following its inception in the United Nations General Assembly in 2014. The approach of Yoga is holistic. It targets the physical, mental, social and spiritual well-being of human beings. It is an ancient practice which was originated in India by its sagas. The Indian Prime Minister, Narendra Modi, in his UN address suggested the date 21 June as it is the longest day of the year in the northern hemisphere and shares a special significance in many parts of the world.

Sages and Rishi of India have devoted their lives to studying multiple abilities, competencies, and health problems of human beings. They gradually evolved an organized system of control by means and methods of which a person could raise his capacities in all directions to their highest level. Yoga has several techniques including physical posturing (asanas), breathing techniques (pranayamas) cleansing technique (kriya) and meditation which have become very popular on account of their application in the improvement of health and total well-being of an individual.

The genesis of yoga can be traced back thousands of years ago. Yoga is a physical, mental, social and spiritual practice that was started by India's ancient sages. They used to practice it to coordinate movements of their mind and body and achieve the highest goals of their lives. There are many varieties of schools, practices and thoughts associated with Yoga. In which two most important segments of yoga, Hath yoga & Raja yoga to which people rely upon most, for instating optimum health. The best thing with both does not only attributive life, but they also detoxify the body physically and mentally in order to maintain the best possible harmony. In succinct words, yoga is a systematic and scientific art of driving and inculcating one's total innate (mind, body, breath & common sense) for unwinding the god gifted attributes. Yoga is a holistic system of providing preventive care and healing psychosomatic disorder without medication.

Today yoga is thought of varied interest, has gained worldwide popularity. Presently researches have shown that it can serve humanity better than anything else. Several components of Yoga such as Yama, Niyama, asana and pranayama can be applied to achieve the physical, mental, social, spiritual health of human beings. It is also useful for cure psychological and functional disorders of people. It is useful for improving performance and productivity. In a nutshell, it has been concluded that yoga in its whole and wide sense is better than any medicine and a psychosomatic disorder correction tool because it prescribes a number of phenomena and substances to tackle diseases in order to realize its long term goal.

Researchers, in the field of the yogic science, have found out that asana, pranayamas and kriyas are the best tools for achieving better goals of human life. They do not only help to develop physical fitness components of the human body but also help to remove its various impediments such as adhivyadhi, roge, asuddi, vighna which are obstacles in the higher spiritual path. Yoga ensures preventive as well as curative values. Practicing yoga makes the body and mind healthy. It is a sort of re-conditioning of the psycho-physiological mechanism of the human body and mind as a whole. It excellently organizes the wholeness of our body in order to find proper equilibrium in its overall functions.

Regular practitioners of yoga become aware of interconnections between human body and mind; intellectual and soul and the aim of yoga, for them, is to fuse gross yogic materials i.e. (five Kosa): Annamaya (physical body), Pranamaya (breathing thought), Manomaya (mental), Vijnanamaya (intellectual) and Anandamaya (spiritual) together to achieve maximum results in the human body.

Height

Human height or stature is the anthropometric variable that is measured in a human body, standing erect from the bottom of feet to the top of the head. It is empirically measured by stadiometer in centimeter or in inches. Height is an important component that plays a major role in deciding our personality in many ways. A specific height is required for selection in armed and police forces as well as certain sports like volleyball and basketball. The factors which decide a person's height are nutritional quantity and quality, physical and mental health, growth of hormones and genetic effects. Genetics among all these is the main factor that affects an individual's height to a great extent. But we, here, are not addressing the impact of that part on height. Lifestyles and psychosomatic disorders also play a major role in deciding height. Having too much anxiety, stress and acidic food like fast food in one's own diet results in dysfunction in the natural growth of the human body. The fear or anxiety, stress, depression as well as acidic food directly affect the individual's tonicity of muscles which affects the gap of the vertebra and decrease the range of movement of the joint and which affects the individual height.

Asanas are practices to make the body and mind healthy and train them in such a way that necessary equilibrium is established in the overall functions of the human body and mind. Asanas recondition the psycho-physiological mechanism of the human body as a whole.

Datta (1993) had conducted research on the comparative effects of yoga and gymnastic programme in the growth pattern of primary school children. 105 children studying in class four and fifth with an average age of10 years were selected as subjects. At the beginning and after 10 months of yoga and gymnastic exercises, their sitting and standing heights were measured. The result showed that the yoga training programme was found to be superior to that of the gymnastic programme in bringing about significant changes in standing height and sitting height of the selected students.

Raghav (2018) had conducted research on the effects of selected yogic practices on height, eye vision and mental well-being among school going children. There were 20 subject aged group between 14 to 17 years. The subjects had to perform yoga practice for 50 minutes for 5 days a week for a period of 12 weeks. The result of the research has shown significant improvement in height, vision and mental well-being.

Kinesthetic sense

Sports scientists, researchers and coaches are doing hard work to optimize the performances of sportsmen in the sporting arena. Kinesthetic ability of sportspersons plays a very instrumental role in deciding their performance. It is useful for learning sports techniques, refinement, modification, and acquirement of new skills during the long term training programme. Kinesthetic ability is the ability to perceive the position, effort and movement of part of the body or the entire body when any muscular action takes place. It is sometimes referred to as the sixth sense. The phrase 'proprioceptive sense' is also used to refer to this sense. The sources of kinesthetic sense are presumably located in the joints, muscles and tendons. Stienhaus (1966) in one of his works, states that individuals who can observe a demonstration and perceive the significance of the sequence of movements are able to develop physical empathy which enables them to learn a movement much faster than other whose kinesthetic ability is not us highly developed. Kinesthetic perception (sense) can be improved through practice. This ability in early childhood is an asset for learning complex skills and techniques in higher stages.

Kinesthetic ability is known as ability of information about body position and movement during any physical movement. It depends on functional ability or capacity of following sensory organ vestibular apparatus of ears, eyes and proprioceptor in muscles and tendons.

Bhomik and Pant (2010) conducted an experiment with the aim to examine "The effect of yogic practices on the psycho-motor variables of physically challenged students". The findings of the research show that the selected yoga practices are useful for physically challenged students in relation to psychomotor variables i.e. eye hand co-ordination, speed and hand steadiness.

On the basis of various research findings, yoga has been found and proved useful for the development of various physical and mental efficiencies of human beings. **Gharote (1987), Bhomik (2010). Desai (1979)** have also revealed that yoga is also helpful for skill development and shooting performance in basketball.

According to Hath yoga, asanas contribute to stability, reduce insomnia (sleepness disorder) improve mental health. In asana, the sympathetic activity is withdrawn and parasympathetic activity restores the stability on various levels that is why the body starts telling the mind through various sensations that are perceived from the proprioceptor and are integrated by the lower center involuntarily. That is why a long-term effect of such performance is seen on the development of attention.

Several investigations have been made to find out the relationship between muscular stress or tension and learning skill task. Beam (1955); Freeman (1933); proposed that muscular tension level, where increased lower the threshold of the higher nervous center, and as a result, simple work capacity is facilitated but complex or accuracy performance may be exhibited.

Memory

Memory is defined by Ryburn (1956) as "the power that we have to store our experiences and to bring them in the field of consciousness sometime after the experiences have occurred". In simple words, memory consists of remembering what has/have already happened. Memory gets affected in different ways because it is not like muscles' training. You can develop your muscles by physical exercise but memory is not helped by any kind of exercise. But it has been witnessed that yogic practices help people to improve their memory by lessening or removing their psychosomatic disorders like stress or tension, anxiety, insomnia and developing self-confidence, attention, concentration and physical, mental, social and spiritual well-being.

Many studies have tried to find the outcome of yoga as a complementary intervention for hypertension, blood pressure, diabetes, insomnia **(Lata, Manju 2002)**.Yoga also improves concentration, reduces anxiety, improves the resting respiratory rate, hemoglobin contents and breath-holding time **(Singh, Samay 2007, Annkili 1993)**.

Naveen et al. (1997) conduct a study to examine the effect of "Yoga breathing through a particular nostril increases spatial memory scores without lateralized effects". In this study 108 subjects were selected whose ages ranged from 10 to 17 years. The findings of the study show significant improvement in all four trained groups, but the control group showed no significant change. The findings of the study showed eighty-four percent average increases in spatial memory scores for the trained group.

Pailoor and Shirley (2009) administered research to look at the effect of two yoga-based relaxation techniques on memory scores and state anxiety. Researchers gave two treatments namely cyclic meditation (CM) and shavasana (SR - supine rest) for a period of 22:30 minutes to seek out results on memory and State anxiety. He made a conclusion of his study that there was a major improvement within the scores of all sections of the Wechsler memory scale and state anxiety studied after both CM and SR but the development shows more after CM compared to SR.

Paqthani, Prof. R.S. and Sah, Sapna (2015), conducted a study and found out that yoga can improve the learning capabilities of school going children. Their study analysed after the experiment that, how yoga affected the learning capabilities i.e. academic, cognitive and psychological, of the students in a school. They calculated their findings by objectively analyzing the available reports, journals and academic research papers and concluded that yoga can significantly improve the learning abilities of school going children.

Mahalinggam, L. et al. (2014) had conducted research on the effects of meditation techniques on selected psychological variables of attention and concentration in women volleyball players. 20 women basketball players of the intercollegiate level were selected from Dr. S.A. College of Physical Education, Triuchendur for a period of 6 weeks. They were the experimental group. For the purpose of the study, the selected psychological variables were concentration and attention and the data were analysed before training and immediately after the training of 6 weeks. The analysis of study results by T-Test at 0.05 level of confidence showed significant changes in pre & post-test of the female volleyball players and their attention and concentration had been significantly improved after the successful completion of the training programme.

Creativity

Creativity is an act of bringing new and imaginative ideas into real action or reality form. Creativity is characterized by the ability to perceive the world in new ways, to find new patterns to make connections between seemingly unrelated or unknown phenomena and to find out the solution of the problem. Creativity has two steps; thinking, and then changing the idea into tangible form. If you have some idea but don't act on them, you can be considered as a person with good imaginative power but not a creative one. Imaginative creation is a process in which something new is produced by converting an idea into an object including. This creative process is carried out either by rearranging the old elements into a new one or by creating something without any sort of imitation. The new creation must contribute to the solution of some problem. Creativity involves the production of useful and novel products. It can be defined as, "the use of imagination or original ideas to create something new". The creative thinker is one who explores new areas and makes new observations, new predictions and new inferences.

Scholars having an interest in creativity include multiple approaches that involve many disciplines such as psychology, sociology, story writing, science and technology. Finding the relationship between creativity and intelligence, personality and creativity ability, creativity and mental health, the relationship of creativity with education and training have been the core areas of interest for the budding researchers who target to contribute to the improvement of the effectiveness of learning and training process. The factors like anxiety, fear, concentration, attention, self-esteem, self-confidence and there inter and intra relationship with creativity have also been very favourable dealt with by several scholars.

Pandya (2014) carried out a study with the aim to examine "the effect of yoga asanas on creativity and memory among school going children" For the purpose of this study 160 subjects whose ages ranged between 11 to 13 years were selected. The training period for this study was 6 weeks (6 days a week). Findings of the study have shown significant enhancement in both variables i.e. creativity and memory.

Albert RS (1999) the term creativity is known as an imaginative idea with a new way into reality. It may be characterized by perceiving the thing or surrounding world in a new way to generate solutions of unrelated phenomena. Creativity has two-step processes thinking and then action for producing. If you have some ideas in your mind but you don't act on them for producing, you may be a good imagination but not creative.

Creativity is what teaches the human to go further, where nobody has gone before. It is the innate desire for naturally creative people to innovate. It brings to our awareness of what was previously hidden and point to new ideas.

Researchers have found that innovation and creativity have a close relationship. Innovation is the implementation of new or significantly improved product service or method of services that create for business, technology, government, or society as whole creativity begins with a foundation of knowledge, learning a discipline and mastering a way of thinking. You learn to be creative by experimenting, exploring, questioning, assumptions using imagination and synthesizing information. There is no innovation without creativity. "The key metric in both creativity and innovation is value creation.

In the present era, schooling and parenting not faster a child's hidden creativity. The educational system has placed a limit on children's initiation in learning rather than spontaneity and creative imagination. In past education systems, creativity was exogenous or purely innate and not everyone needed to be creative. A child is most of the time introduced only to the learning process by schooling and family but not to the creative process. Creativity may be encouraged in a variety of ways and art are a dynamic channel to foster a child's creativity. For enhancing creativity collaborative projects and demonstrate are the power of collaborative creativity. For developing creativity by schooling system includes emphasis process rather than a product, provide a classroom environment that allows children to explore and play without under restraints adapt to children's ideas rather than trying to structure for children's ideas

Statement of the Problem

The problem was stated that "A Study on effects of Selected Yogic Practices (Suryanamaskar, Asanas, Pranayama, Kriya, Yoga Nidra) on Height, Kinesthetic Sense, Memory, and Creativity among School Going Children".

Objective of the Study

- To analyze the effect of yogic practices on height.
- To analyze the effect of yogic practices on kinesthetic sense.
- To analyze the effect of yogic practices on memory.
- To analyze the effect of yogic practices on creativity.

Hypothesis

Ho1: It was hypothesized that yogic practices would not have any significant repercussions in Height among school going children.

Ho2: It was hypothesized that yogic practices would not have any significant repercussions in Kinesthetic sense among school going children.

Ho3 It was hypothesized that yogic practices would not have any significant repercussions in Memory among school going children.

Ho4: It was hypothesized that yogic practices would not have any significant repercussions in Creativity among school going children.

Delimitations of the study

1. This study was delimited to only male students as the research subjects.

2. Area of research was confined to Brilliant Public School, Aligarh district of Uttar Pradesh.

3. A study was done on sixty students of the age group of 14-17 years old.

4. Height, Kinesthetic Sense, Memory, and Creativity were considered as the Dependent variable of the study.

5. Selected Yogic Practices in which (Suryanamaskar, Asanas, Pranayamas, kriya and Yoga Nidra) were taken as Independent Variables.

Limitations of the study

1. The socio-economic and cultural status of the students was not taken into consideration.

2. The researcher had no control over certain factors like diet, routine work; environment etc and they were not taken into consideration.

3. The stress, strain of personal habits and their state of mind may be another limitation for the study.

Definition and Explanation of the Important Terms

Yoga

योगश्चित्तवृत्तिनिरोधः "yogashchittavrittinirodhah"

The great sage Patanjali's famous definition of yoga is "yogashchittavrittinirodhah", It means yoga bring harmony to the body and mind through get rid of the unwanted impulses generated in the mind.

It is a mental, physical and spiritual discipline which focuses on bringing harmony between body and mind. It is an art and science of healthy living.

Asanas

The asanas can only be defined as the 'postural pattern'. One has to achieve this pattern slowly, maintain for some time steadily and to release it again in a slow and smooth manner.

Pranayama

Pranayama means a voluntary and temporary pause in the movement of breath.

"Tasmin sati shvasa-prashvasyor-gati-vichchhedahpranayamah" Patanjal Yoga

sutra 2:49. The meaning is that the pause, brought in the movement of inhalation and exhalation, is nothing but pranayamas.

Yoga nidra

It is a temperament of the body being fully unstrained in which the subject achieves up - stair and gradual awareness of the inner world by following verbal instructions on various body segments.

Height

Height is the measurement of someone or something from head to foot or from base to top. It is a measurement of a person or thing. The distance from the bottom to top of something standing upright, especially the distance from the lowest to the highest point of a body especially of human being.

Kinesthetic sense

Kinesthetic sense is the sense which helps us detect weight, body position or the relationship between movements in our body parts such as joints, muscles and tendons. In short, it is the muscle sense or we can say sense of body awareness.

Memory

"Memory consists in remembering what has previously been learnt".

Memory is the process by which information is encoded, stored and retrieved. Encoding allows information from the outside world to be sensed in the form of chemical and physical stimuli. Storage is the secondary memory process and allows for the creation of a stable, more permanent record of encoded information. Finally, the third process is the retrieval of information that has been stored. Such information must be accessed and returned to consciousness or working memory. Depending on the type of information stored, retrieval may be effortless or it may require a more cognitively demanding search through memory.

Creativity

Creativity is the tendency to generate or recognize ideas, alternatives, or possibilities that may be useful in solving problems, communicating with others, and entertaining ourselves and others.

Creativity is a phenomenon whereby something new and somehow valuable is formed. The created item may be intangible (such as an idea, a scientific theory, a musical composition, or a joke) or a physical object (such as an invention, a literary work, or a painting).

Significances of the Study

The ultimate of this study would manifest the outcome of selected (Yoga Asana, Pranayama, Kriya, and Yoga Nidra) on the male students for height, kinesthetic sense, memory, and creativity.

The study would draw a systematic and scientific foundation for players, coaches, and physical educationists on comprehensive knowledge for selected (Yoga Asana, Pranayama, Kriya, and Yoga Nidra) and their effects on height, kinesthetic sense, memory, and creativity.

This study would unlock various dimensions of scope to the physical educationist for conducting further research on height, kinesthetic sense, memory, and creativity.

The result of this study would add on some important horizons of knowledge to support new studies related to sports psychology, sports training and exercise physiology.

Chapter II

REVIEW OF RELATED LITERATURE

Raghav (2018) had conducted research on the effects of selected yogic practices on height, eye vision and mental well-being among school going children. There were 20 subject aged group between 14 to 17 years. The subjects had to perform yoga practice for 50 minutes for 5 days in a week for a period of 12 weeks. Result of the research has shown significant improvement in height, vision and mental well-being.

Kumar (2018) had conducted research on the effects of selected yogic practices on Psycho – Physiological variables on male students. There were 30 subject aged group between 14 to 18 years. The subjects had to perform yoga practice for 60 minutes for 5 days in a week for a period of 3 months. Result of the research has shown significant improvement in mental health, personality, self-concept, blood pressure, respiratory rate, vital capacity, pulse rate, breathing holding time.

Rejinadevi & Ramesh (2017) conducted research work to scrutinize the "Effect of Yogic Practices on selected physiological variables among basketball players". For this study, forty male basketball players, aged between 18 to 25 were selected as subjects from Nadar Mahajana Sangam S. Vellaichamy Nadar College, Madurai, Tamilnadu. They were randomly divided into two groups of twenty players in each group namely the experimental group and control group. This study was conducted for a period of 12 weeks. During this study, the experimental group performed yogic activities and also did their regular activities of the college. While the control group players did their regular college activities in the same period. A sphygmomanometer was used to measure their systolic and diastolic blood pressure. The results showed that there was a significant improvement in the experimental group on selected criterion variables (systolic blood pressure, diastolic blood pressure) in comparison to the control group.

Mitchell et al. (2015) conducted a research on mindfulness meditation training for Attention- Deficit/ Hyperactivity Disorder in adulthood. The researcher explored that mindfulness based training program is an example of intervention that is attaining promising preliminary empirical supports and is increasingly administered in clinical settings. The aim of the study was to give a rationale for the uses of mindfulness to individual diagnosed with ADHD, and summarize a treatment approach to adults diagnosed with ADHD. The results also revealed the directions for the further researches in future that include the mindfulness meditation as a standalone treatment and as a complementary approach to cognitive behavioral therapy.

Bilderbeck et al. (2013) conducted a research on prison population to assess the effects of 10-week yoga course on behavioural control improvement and reduction of psychological distress. The study reveals that yoga was effective in reducing the symptoms of anxiety and depression. The study also revealed that yoga may improve control and cognitive- behavioural performance. Participants who were administered with yoga showed positive effects, and reduction of stress and psychological distress in comparison to those participants who was under the control group. Participants who administered with yoga also showed good performance in the cognitive-behavioural task. The study concluded that subjective well-being and mental health among prison population can be improved by yoga.

Telles S, Singh N, Balkrishna A. et al. (2013) made a study on " The effect of yoga or physical exercise on physical, cognitive and emotional measures in children". For the purpose of this study 98 randomized subjects aged between 8 to 13 years were divided into physical exercise and yoga groups.

The tests used for the analysis were

1)   The teacher's rating of the children's attention, punctuality, obedience, academic and behaviour with their friends and teachers.
2)   Eurofit physical test
3)   Stroop colour-word task test and
4)   Battles self –esteem inventory test.

The yoga programme consisted (postures, breathing, technique, chanting and guided relaxation). It was conducted for a period of 45 min. for 5 days in a week. In the same period, other groups performed relay races, jogging on the spot, rapid repetitive movements or games. After completion of 3 months, the two groups were assessed. Social self-esteem was found to be significantly higher in physical exercise group compared to yoga group (p<0.05). In both groups, researcher found an increase in B.M.I. and no. of sit-ups. Physical exercise group showed poor balance while yoga group had enhanced plate tapping. Both groups had a significantly better word and colour word naming. Furthermore, studies showed an enhanced total and parental self-esteem in yoga group. Both kinds of activities were found to be effective and helpful in regular school activities. This study is registered by the Trials Registry of India.

Rocha et al. (2012) studied that yoga is believed to have positive effects on cognition, attenuation of emotional intensity and stress reduction. The author explored the effects of yoga on memory and psychological parameters related to stress, comparing yoga practice and physical exercises in men. They assessed in study variables before or after 6 months of yoga practice. Researchers concluded that yoga practice can increase aspects of cognition and quality of life for individuals and it also can improve emotional state on cognition.

Kumar et al. (2011) studied the effect of yogic pranayama and meditation on selected physical and physiological variables. Thirty boys in the age group of 12 to 15 years were selected from Karnataka university, department of yoga, Dharwad. The subjects were divided into two groups namely control group and experimental The Experimental group was given yogic pranayama and meditation for a period of twelve weeks in both morning and evening sessions on alternative days in a week. The control group did not participate in yogic pranayama and meditation training program. The collected data were statistically analyzed by using analysis of covariance (ANCOVA). The experimental group had a significant improvement on the selected physical and physiological variables except systolic and diastolic Blood pressure than that of control group.

Bhomik and Pant (2010) conducted an experiment with the aim to examine "The Effect of Yogic Practices on the psycho-motor variables of physically challenged students". Subjects selected from Amar Jyoti School and Rehabilitation Centre Gwalior, Madhya Pradesh, India their age range between 8-15 years, forty subjects were chosen for this study. The training period of this study was scheduled five days a week for duration of 45 minutes each day for 6 weeks and was progressively extended to 60 minutes on a weekly basis. Subjects were randomly divided into control and experimental groups. Each group had an equal sample size of twenty subjects. The selected psychomotor variables were recorded on pre-test and post-test. Data on psychomotor variables were recorded with the assistance of ordinary procedures like Speed of movement test by Nelson and Johnson's, Hand steadiness by hand steadiness tester and Eye-hand coordination by mirror tracking test. In order to know the effect of yogic exercise on the selected psychomotor variables, covariance technique was used to find out the results at a 0.05 level of significance. In this study researcher notice that F-ratio was found to be significant for all the selected psychomotor characteristics i.e. Speed of movement. Hand steadiness and Eye-Hand Coordination in comparison to the control group at a 0.05 level of significance. The findings of the study showed that the selected yoga practices are useful for physically challenged students.

Chidambara Raja (2010) made a study on "The Effects of yogic practice and physical fitness on flexibility, anxiety and blood pressure". Forty-five subjects were selected for this study, all working women in the age group of 35 to 40 years in various faculties of Annamalai University. Forty-five subjects were divided into three equal groups of 15 subjects in each group. Yogic practice Group for Yogic activities, physical exercise group was for physical activities and control group acted as control who didn't participate in any training programme. The training session was held five days a week for a period of eight weeks. Variables like Flexibility was measured by sit and reach test, anxiety by Taylor's Manifest Anxiety scale and pressure level was measured by sphygmomanometer. All groups were tested before and after eight weeks of the training period, the researcher tested flexibility, anxiety and pressure level (systolic and diastolic). The information was analyzed statistically by using the "Analysis of Co- Variance" (ANCOVA). This study suggested that there was a significant improvement among the experimental group on selected variables (flexibility, systolic blood pressure, diastolic blood pressure) as compared to the control group.

Kloubec (2010) conducted research work to scrutinize the effect of Pilates exercise for improvement of muscle endurance, flexibility, balance and posture. The aim of the study was to work out the consequences of Pilates exercise on abdominal endurance, hamstring flexibility, upper- body muscular endurance, posture, and balance. For the aim of the study, fifty subjects engaged to participate in a twelve-week. The class was given to subjects for one hour two times per week. Subjects were randomly divided into either the experimental (n=25) or control group (n=25). At the last of the twelve-week period, a one-way analysis of covariance result showed a significant level of enhancement (p< 0.05) in endurance and flexibility but posture and balance did not improve. The result of the study shows that individuals can improve their muscular endurance and flexibility using relatively low-intensity Pilates exercises do not need a high degree of skill and equipment and are easy to master and use within a personal fitness routine.

Ross, A. and Thomas, S. (2010) conduct a study on the Health Benefits of Yoga and Exercise. Exercise is taken into account to be a suitable method for improving and maintaining physical and emotional health. A growing body of evidence supports the belief that yoga benefits physical and psychological state via down regulation of the hypothalamic–pituitary–adrenal (HPA) axis and also the sympathetic systema nervosum (SNS). The aim of this text is to supply a scholarly review of the literature regarding research studies comparing the results of yoga and exercise on a variety of health outcomes and health conditions. Within the studies reviewed, yoga interventions gave the impression to be equal or superior to exercise in nearly every outcome measured except those involving fitness. The studies comparing the consequences of yoga and exercise seem to point that, in both healthy and diseased populations; yoga could also be as effective as or better than exercise at improving a range of health-related outcome measures. Future clinical trials are needed to look at the distinctions between exercise and yoga, particularly how the 2 modalities may differ in their effects on the SNS=HPA axis. Further studies using rigorous methodologies are needed to appear at the health benefits of the numerous varieties of yoga.

Sukla and Singh (2010) made a study to research Yoga for Stress Relief. Yogic Practices well demonstrated to cut back the physical effect of stress on the body and has even been found to decrease cortisol levels. Subjects find that they feel more relax after yogic practicing. The yoga asanas practicing are more helpful for reducing muscular tension, which helps to scale back stress. we've got an inclination to store stress not only in our systema nervosum but distributed throughout the musculature, systema digestorium and other tissues of the body as an example they responses very quickly to worry Yoga may be a beneficial and effective tool for recovering from the after effects of traumatic event. Yoga reduces stress by acting on several different levels-mental, emotional, physical and even spiritual to calm the body and also the mind.

Singh, R. (2010) carried out a study to examine the effect of certain yogic asanas and physical exercises on balance ability. Healthy adults were divided into four groups i.e. experimental group 'A', 'B', 'C' and control group 'D' of 20 subjects each, total subjects were eighty. The aim of this study was to examine the response of certain asanas and exercise programme on balance ability and to assess their effectiveness as measured by BASS-STRICK test (cross-wise), Johnson and Nelson (1988). The analysis of information revealed that the three experimental groups trained by exercise, asanas and combined exercise and asanas, showed significant improvement in performance of balance ability but the mean gain achieved by combined exercise and yogic asanas groups was better than exercise group and control group.

Singh, R. (2010) administered a study with the aim to look at the effect of certain yogic asanas and physical exercises on kinesthetic ability. subjects were randomly selected age ranged in-between 19-21 years, total eighty subjects were selected for this study and divided into four groups namely exercise group, yogic group, combined group and control group. The experimental groups went for twelve weeks of treatment programme; both pre and post-test were collected for analysis of the information. the information collection was made on kinesthetic ability test by arms raising test suggested by Scott. The results of analysis of covariance (Ancova) showed a significant difference all told the groups except the control group. Between the combined and yoga group, exercise group and yoga group, a major difference in paired adjusted final mean is seen. The asana group was obtained most significant than other groups.

Sharma S.K. (2010) applied a study with the aim of measuring the "Effect of Yogic Practices, Physical Exercises and Combination of Yogic Practices and Physical Exercises on Selected Motor Ability Components, Physiological and Psychological Variables of Senior Gymnasium Boys in Delhi". For the aim of the study 160 subjects had been randomly selected. They were divided into four groups namely Yogic group (40 subjects) and physical exercises group (40subjects), a combination of yogic practices and physical exercises group (40) and control group (40). The age of subjects ranged from16 to 18 years. Experimental groups underwent their respective training programme for a period of six weeks. The parameter studied included selected motor ability components (cardiorespiratory endurance, flexibility), physiological (Breath-holding time, resting pulse rate), Psychological (Anxiety, Mental Concentration) variables etc. The results were compared with control group before and at the tip of the training programme after six weeks. Results show significant improvement in physiological variables, psychological variables and motor ability components variables. Hence, this study suggested that yogic exercises, physical exercises and a combination of physical exercises and yogic practices are very useful for a person's.

Pailoor and Shirley (2009) Undertook research with the aim to examine the effect of 2 yoga relaxation techniques on state anxiety and memory scores. A yoga practice involving cycles of yoga asanas and supine relaxation (called cyclic meditation) was previously shown to boost performance in attention tasks more than corpse posture (Shavasana). For this study 57 male volunteer' subjects, whose average age ± S.D., 26.6 ± 4.5 years. In this study, the immediate effect of C.M. and S.R. was assessed on state anxiety and memory. Subjects were examined after and before (i) C.M.one day and (ii) S.R. on another day, both practiced for twenty-two minutes and thirty seconds for an equal duration. (i) attention and concentration (digit span forward and backward) were assessed by the Wechsler memory scale (WMS) (ii) State anxiety was assessed using Spielberger's state-trait anxiety Inventory (STAI). After the analysis of the data, results show that there was an enhancement in the scores of all sections of the WMS, but the results showed more improvement after (C.M.) in comparison with (S.R.) State anxiety decreased after both (C.M.) and (S R) but more score decrease after (C.M.). A cyclical combination of yoga asana and supine rest in CM improved memory scores immediately after the practice and decreased state anxiety more than rest during a yoga relaxation asana (Shavasana).

Ganguly, S. K. (2009) Yogic practices are psychophysical because their effects are both on body and mind. Asanas can be called as postural pattern. Maharshi Patanjali has given one or two sutras about Asanas. Even in this we get indication that Asanas are psychophysical. Asana is postural pattern, which is stable and comfortable. We can rather say Asanas create stability and Sukha. Asanas bring stability, feeling of well-being and lightness/suppleness. After Asanas, practice of Pranayama is suggested which requires sitting stable for a long time. Later on other Asanas could have been added. The main criterion meditative Practices: is to sit comfortably for a long time. Forget body consciousness in that comfortable pose. Cultural Practices are very often undue in numbering. Cultural Asanas are to keep well-being going. These Asanas cannot be pushed back more than mediaeval age. Hathayoga Pradipika describes fifteen and Gheranda Samhita describes thirty two Asanas. Relaxative Practices is to relax the systems which have accumulated fatigue. Body Works smoothly when different systems work smoothly. Asanas like Dhanurasana, Bhujangasana and Shalabhasana etc. help a lot in this regard. Uddiyana, Nauli help the diaphragm to be raised thereby giving good massage from downward to the heart. Practices like Bhujangasana, Dhanurasana, Salabhasana alternatively exert pressure on heart. For better health, three conditions are to be fulfilled. They are healthy respiratory muscles with elasticity wherein no air cell should remain idle and cleansed respiratory passage. In this context, Nauli, Uddiyana and Kapalabhati help a lot to build-up respiratory muscles powerful. Deep inspiration in Shalabhasana and Dhanurasana and deep expiration in Uddiyana and Nauli help to build up elastic respiratory muscles while Kapalabhati cleanses the respiratory passage forcefully. The practices especially like Shirshasana, Viparitakarani, and Sarvangasana work wonderfully for better venous return. These Asanas are not available in Physical Exercise programme or even in "sports. Although cases like adenoids, deviated septum, populous cannot be tackled but some Asanas and other practices that can deal with tonsils are Viparitakarani, Sarvangasana, Matsyasana, Simhamudra, and Jihva 'Bandha. There are number of deference between asanas and exercise as because 'the very principle differs. It improves mental, emotional health, improves circulation and cardiac health. Blood flows to heart and improves when unhealthy factors removed; heart grows new blood vessels (natural "bypass"). Research studies done on selected Asanas upon School boys, girls, Indian Police cadets, showed good changes in health and fitness. Yogic practices as a whole provide psycho-physiological balance (i.e. Homeostasis) in improving Autonomic unactions. Crimes are the acts which are forbidden and punished by law; these acts may threaten the well-being of the society, or injure any of its members. People are most likely to commit a criminal act between the age of 15 and 25 years. Imprisonment is a method of dealing with the people who commits crimes by confining them to a fortified boundary with a certain strict rules for all that in the prison. Crimes like any other action of the body are a manifestation of thought. Crimes come to be regarded as essentially a social problem and retribution as the object of improvement is discarded. Detention as an objective in imprisonment is also very limited in scope. Reformation of the offender is being regarded as an ultimate aim of the prison sentence. Rehabilitation of the criminals has become one of the most important objective of the jail authorities. Apart from the criminal aspect many inmates manifest mental disorders in prison as a result of stresses of incarceration. The stresses behind the bars include separation from their family members, overcrowding sensory deprivation, and exposure to high density of hard core offenders and variety of uncertainty, fear and frustration. The period of trial is of great stress to the individual. Loss of status, uncertainty of the outcome of the trial, fear of punishment staying in a usual place like police station or jail and the financial upset harasses the individual. If trial period is prolonged for months or years, which is very common, then the under trial's condition become badly. The hard life in the prison further aggravates the situation. The under trial's quality of life and subjective well-being are seriously affected by aforesaid conditions in the prison. Psychological factors like anxiety, aggression and personality might be cause or the consequence of criminal behaviour and in some cases both. Prison's reforms measures should lead to some reduction in inmates feeling of hostility, helplessness and other negative emotions.

Avalle and Vallumurgan (2008) conducted a study with the purpose of measuring the effects of selected yogic exercise and psychological skill training on selected psycho physiological and psychomotor variables of high- level participants. In order to achieve the purpose of the present study, forty five inter-collegiate level players from Maruthi College of Physical Education, Coimbatore were randomly selected as subjects in between the age group of 18 to 24 years. The study was formulated as a really random group design, consisting of a pre-test and a post-test. The forty-five subjects were randomly divided into three equal groups namely psychological skills training group (PST), yogic exercises group (YE) and control group (CG). Each group consisted of fifteen subjects. The variables selected were cognitive anxiety, self-confidence, heart rate, systolic blood pressure, diastolic blood pressure and body temperature as psycho-physiological variables and reaction time, and hand eye co-ordination as psychomotor variables. The psychological skills training group and yogic exercises group participated in pre-decided activities for a period of twelve weeks and the post tests were conducted. Analysis of covariance statistical technique was accustomed test the adjusted mean difference among the three groups. When the adjusted post – test was significant, the Scheffe post hoc test was accustomed find out the paired mean differences. By analysis of covariance the cognitive anxiety was significant at 0.05 levels with F ratio of 9.66 as the table F ratio was 3.23 for adjusted means. By analysis of covariance the self-confidence was significant at 0.05 level with a ratio of 29.78 as the table F ratio was 3.23 for adjusted means. By analysis of covariance the heart rate was significant at 0.05 level with an F ration of 1.85 as the table F ratio was 3.23 for adjusted means. By analysis of covariance the systolic blood pressure was insignificant at 0.05 level with F ratio of0.96 as the table F ratio was 3.23 for adjusted mean. By analysis of covariance the hand eye co- ordination was significant at 0.05 levels with F ratio of 1032.81 as the table F ratio was 3.23 for adjusted means. By analysis of covariance the reaction time was significant at 0.05 levels with F of 13.76 as the table F ratio 3.23 for adjusted means by analysis of covariance the body temperature was insignificant at 0.05 levels with F ratio of 1.28 and the table F ratio was 3.23 for adjusted means. The results of the study show that there were significant differences in cognitive anxiety, somatic anxiety, self-confidence, and heart rate due to the influence of yogic exercises and psychological skills training. In case of diastolic blood pressure, systolic blood pressure and body temperature there were insignificant differences due to yogic exercises and psychological skills training. The results of the study shown that there was a significant difference in the hand eye coordination and reaction time due to influence of yogic exercises and psychological skills training. The result of the study showed that there was a significant difference in the self-confidence and hand eye co-ordination between the yogic exercises and psychological skills training group.

Muthukumar (2007) administered a study with the aim of measuring the effect of yogic practices on the development of fitness skills among the mentally retarded boys. Sixty mentally retarded boys were selected from CSI mentally retarded school, Sivakasi. They were randomly divided into two groups experimental group and control group. Experimental group was involved in Yogic Practices programme for 6 weeks and also the subjects in control group weren't engaged in any physical activity during this duration. The information were statistically analyzed by using analysis of covariance (ANCOVA). Experimental group had a major improvement in their fitness skills than the control group.

Preetha (2006) administrated the study to search out the "effect of selected yoga asanas and aerobic exercises on selected physical, physiological and psychological variables among women students" of Pondicherry University. Selected subjects were randomly divided into three equal groups consisting of 1 control and two experimental groups, subject ages were in between 20 to 25 years. the primary Experimental group underwent aerobic exercises; experimental group second underwent yoga asana practice. The training session was held five days every week for a period of 12 weeks. Control group wasn't engaged in any physical activity during this duration. before and at the tip of training period, all subjects were tested for selected physical, physiological and psychological variables. Aerobic exercises and yoga practice group showed significant enhancement on selected physical, physiological and psychological variables like weight, flexibility, and balance among experimental group than the control group.

Brown and Gerbarg (2005) discover in their study that Yogic breathing a powerful method for balancing the autonomic nervous system and influencing psychological and stress-related disorders. Part I of this series has presented a neurophysiologic theory of the results of Sudarshan Kriya Yoga (SKY) and part II has presented clinical studies, our own clinical observations and guidelines for the safe and effective use of yoga breathing techniques during a large selection of clinical conditions. there's sufficient evidence to think about Sudarshan Kriya Yoga to be a beneficial, low-risk, low-cost adjunct to the treatment of stress, anxiety, post-traumatic stress disorder (PTSD), depression, stress-related medical illnesses, habit, and rehabilitation of criminal offenders. SKY has been used as a public health intervention to alleviate PTSD in survivors of mass disasters. Yoga techniques enhance well-being, mood, attention, mental focus, and stress tolerance. Proper training by a trained teacher on a each day for a duration of 30-minute would maximize the advantages of the subjects. Yoga trainer plays a crucial role in encouraging patients to remain up their yoga practices.

Sharma and Sharma (2004) conducted a study on attitude of an individual that is the way of thinking and perceiving the things around us. It is resultant of our belief, knowledge, daily practice and social environment. An individual's attitude keeps us very happy in any situation. This study examined the effect of yogic training on the attitude of school going students. 30 Male subjects age ranging between 10 to 16 years was selected by stratified random sampling technique form Ramjas Sec. School No. 5, Karol Bagh, New Delhi. After the successful training of the yogic training' a psychological test namely (Sodhi's Attitude Scales) has been applied to measure the attitude of the students. The test includes (i) Attitude towards teachers and parents (ii) Attitude towards discipline, (iii) Attitude towards life and humanity, (iv) Attitude towards country. (v) Attitude towards religion. The result of study showed that most of the subject (80% subject) improved their Attitude towards teachers and parents. The result of study shows that most of the subject (70% subject) improved their Attitude towards Discipline. The result of study Shows that most of the subject (90% subject) improved their Attitude towards Life and Humanity. The result of study Shows that most of the subject (80% subject) improved their Attitude towards Country. The result of study Shows that most of the subject (90% subject) improved their Attitude towards Religion.

West et al. (2004) conducted an experiment with the aim to examine some of the psychological and neuroendocrine response to certain activities. Sixty-nine healthy college students participated in one of the following three 90-min classes: African dance (n = 21), Hatha yoga (n= 18), or a biology lecture as a control session (n = 30). Before and after each condition, the participants completed the Perceived Stress Scale (PSS), the Positive Affect and Negative Affect Schedule and provided a saliva sample for cortisol. There were significant reductions in PSS and negative affect (ps< .0001) and Time x Treatment interactions (ps< .0001) such that African dance and Hatha yoga showed significant declines, whereas there was no significant change in biology lecture. There was a significant main effect for salivary cortisol (p < .05) and a significant interaction effect (p < .0001) such that cortisol increased in African dance, decreased in Hatha yoga, and did not change in biology. Changes in cortisol were not significantly related to changes in psychological variables across treatments. Both African dance and Hatha yoga reduced perceived stress and negative effect. Cortisol increased in African dance and decreased in Hatha yoga. Therefore, even when these interventions produce similar positive psychological effects, the effects may be very different on physiological stress processes. One factor that may have particular salience is that amount of physiological arousal produced by the intervention.

Dalal (2002) reveals that emotion is a motive power which helps in our evolution. In yogic terminology, emotion is a Rajas guna of Prakriti which exists in everyone. Excitement or upsurge of emotion is responsible for many types of disease. Psycho physiologically, emotions act upon our body through hypothalamus, which controls ANS and the endocrine systems. Negative emotions like anger, fear, greed, jealousy give rise to somatic illness where on the other hand positive emotions like love, compassion, friendship, affection etc. give the strength to combat the stress. Illness due to negative emotions includes hyper acidity, hypertension, insomnia, menstrual disturbances, loss of appetite etc. Daily yoga sadhana of eight-fold path with a proper balanced diet helps one to act against stressful threshold situations by increasing the threshold of tolerance. The beauty of yoga therapy is that it treats the individual as a whole. An observation was made on 287 sadhakas (male=133 and female=154). Their financial condition, family background and environment were noted. Different symptoms of the subjects were tabulated and studied for every 2 months with the help of physical check-ups and psychological testing with different questionnaires related to anxiety, depression, positive and negative outlook towards life. All the findings were again tabulated in details. The variables stated above were tested before and after the programmes viz. Pratipakshabhavana, Anityabhavana and Sakshibhavana respectively. These practices were done daily for a period of 2 months. The favorable results suggest that Yoga leads to Samadhi, kaivalya, eternal bliss which aim to maintain physical fitness, mental stability, emotional quietness and spiritual elevation.

James and Raub (2002) examined that yoga has become increasingly popular in Western cultures as a means of exercise and fitness training; however, it is still depicted as trendy as evidenced by an April 2001 Time magazine cover story on "The Power of Yoga." There is a need to have yoga better recognized by the health care community as a complement to conventional medical care. Over the last 10 years, a growing number of research studies have shown that the practice of Hatha Yoga can improve strength and flexibility, and may help control such physiological variables as blood pressure, respiration and heart rate, and metabolic rate to improve overall exercise capacity. This review presents a summary of medically substantiated information about the health benefits of yoga for healthy people and for people compromised by musculoskeletal and cardiopulmonary disease

Ray, U. S. et al. (2001) made a study on effects of yogic asanas and physical exercise on body flexibility in middle aged men. 54 trainees of 20-25 years age group were divided randomly in two groups i.e. yoga and control group. Yoga group (23 males and 5 females) was administered yogic practices for the first five months of the course while control group (21 males and 5 females) did not perform yogic exercises during this period. From the 6th to 10th month of training both the groups performed the yogic practices. Physiological parameters like heart rate, blood pressure, oral temperature, skin temperature in resting condition, responses to maximal and sub maximal exercise, body flexibility were recorded. Psychological parameters like personality, learning, arithmetic and psychomotor ability, mental well-being was also recorded. Various parameters were taken before and during the 5th and 10th month of training period. Initially there was relatively higher sympathetic activity in both the groups due to the new work/training environment but gradually it subsided. Later on at the 5th and 10th month, yoga group had relatively lower sympathetic activity than the control group. There was improvement in performance at sub maximal level of exercise and in anaerobic threshold in the yoga group. Shoulder, hip, trunk and neck flexibility improved in the yoga group. There was improvement in various psychological parameters like reduction in anxiety and depression and a better mental function after yogic practices.

Rajmohan (2001) conducted a research on the effect of yoga asanas on memory, attention, achievement motivation and scholastic achievement of primary school children. The findings of the research revealed that an effective yoga model played a prominent role for improving memory, attention, achievement and motivation and guide to improved learning achievement. The variables which are selected for this study are related to the learning process and they streamline the processing of information thereby facilitating better learning. It had been found that yoga practices improve attention, memory, and achievement motivation and enhance scholastic achievements among the primary students. Hence the curriculum designers and education planners should play an important role in restructuring the curriculum to provide a right place for Yoga. Youth of this country should be physically and mentally powerful enough to make our nation strong and more powerful. The right way to achieve this is to provide education in tune with our national values and aspirations.

Naveen et al. (1997) conducted a study on Yoga breathing through a particular nostril increases spatial memory scores without lateralized effects. Uninostril breathing facilitates the performance on spatial and verbal cognitive tasks. Since hemispheric memory functions are also known to be lateralized, the present study assessed the effects of uninostril breathing on the performance in verbal and spatial memory tests. School children (N = 108 whose ages ranged from 10 to 17 years) were randomly assigned to four groups. Each group practiced a specific yoga breathing technique: (i) right nostril breathing, (ii) left nostril breathing, (iii) alternate nostril breathing, or (iv) breath awareness without manipulation of nostrils. These techniques were practiced for 10 days. Verbal and spatial memory was assessed initially and after 10 days. An age-matched control group of 27 were similarly assessed. All 4 trained groups showed a significant increase in spatial test scores at retest, but the control group showed no significant change. Average increase in spatial memory scores for the trained groups was 84%. It appears yoga breathing increases spatial rather than verbal scores, without a lateralized effect.

Sakthignanavel (1995) determined the effect of continuous running, yogic pranayama, and combination of continuous running and yogic pranayamic exercises on cardio-respiratory endurance, selected physiological and psychological variables. In this study sixty male school students were randomly selected and divided into four groups. Group I practiced continuous running. Group II performed Pranayama practice, Group III performed, the combined continuous running and Pranayama practice and Group IV served as the control group and was not involved in any kind of training. In each group, subjects were trained with respective programmes for 14 weeks, 4 times a week, each training session lasted for thirty minutes. Previous to and at the end of the training period, all groups were tested for cardio-respiratory endurance, selected physiological and psychological variables. Combined continuous running & yogic Pranayama group showed significant development on cardio-respiratory endurance & psychological variables & some of the physiological

Variables excepting cardiac variables like systolic pressure, diastolic pressure, pulse pressure, mean pressure, & rate pressure product.

Schell, et al. (1994) carried out a study on physiological and psychological effects of Hatha – Yoga exercise on healthy women. They measured blood pressure, heart rate, prolactin, the hormones cortisol, and growth hormone and certain psychological parameters in a yoga practicing group and a control group of young female volunteers prior and after the training period. There were no overall differences between the groups concerning blood pressure and endocrine parameters. The heart rate was significantly different in yoga group having a significant reduces in heart rate during the yogic training programme. In the personality inventory, the yoga group showed noticeably higher scores in life satisfaction and lower scores in excitability, aggressiveness, openness, emotionality and somatic complaints. Markedly differences could also be observed concerning coping with stress and mood at the end of the experiment. The yoga group had significantly greater scores in high spirits and extra variedness.

Byrne and Byrne (1993) had thoroughly examined 30 studies related to effect of exercise on depression, anxiety and other mood states. Investigations of their study were supportive of the anti-depressant, anti-anxiety and mood enhancing effects of exercise programs. The benefits of exercise on depression, anxiety and other states of disturbed mood were examined in study. Overall, the report suggested that the research supports the notion that exercise has psychological benefits for participants. In addition, the studies which was examined generally substantiate the claim that improved mood is associated with exercise. A non-aerobic activity was found to have equally better effects on the alleviation of depression as an aerobic activity (running) suggested that positive effects on mood resulting from exercise may not be dependent on an increase in aerobic capacity. Finally, the authors suggested that the relation between improvements in fitness and improvements in mood require more thorough investigation.

Indirani (1993) conducted a study on the "Effects of yoga asanas on selected physical, physiological and psychological variables among school boys". Results of the study suggested that the effects of yoga asanas were significant on elasticity of muscle and suppleness. The Pranayama significantly improved breath holding capacity (BHC), vital capacity (VC) resting pulse rate (RPR).

Janowiak (1993) conducted a study on the effects of meditation on college students and their self-actualization and stress management. This study conducted to determine the efficiency of meditation in promoting self-actualization among college students and to ascertain whether practice of meditation produces changes in subjective levels of stress. And the study suggested that training of meditation provides greater improvement in systematically relaxed behaviour at the end of the relaxation training but does not show significant effectiveness in promoting positive personality changes

Barnes and Nagarker (1989) in their research work entitled Yoga Education Scholastic Achievement found a positive effect of yogic practices on academic achievements. This study was conducted on 40 students selected from school registers of VIII standard (age group 13-15 years) on the basis of their willingness to participate in yoga training camp for four months. The schedule consisted of Asana, Pranayama and Kriyas for 2 hours every day. For data collection Scholastic Aptitude Test and Non-verbal Test were administered before and after yoga training camp. The results have reflected a significant positive effect of yoga training camp on scholastic aptitude as well as on intelligence.

Berger and David (1988) conducted a study on stress reduction and mood enhancement with the help of four activities; swimming, body conditioning, hatha yoga and fencing. Students voluntarily enrolled in co-educational fencing, body conditioning, swimming and yoga administered the POMS, a measure of mood states and the state anxiety subscale of the STM before and after class on three different days, students were significantly more fatigued than before. In body conditioning, the interaction between pre and post means was significant. Yoga participants felt significantly better after exercising on four POMS subscales.

Kalayil (1988) has compared the effects of yoga meditation (YM), Progressive Relaxation Training (PRT), Catnap (CAT) and the control Group Magazine Reading (MAG) in reducing the state anxiety and heart rate as well as relieving headaches, insomnia and general tension. In this study, stress was viewed as tension. In this study stress was viewed as a multi-dimensional experience with physiological, behavioral and psychological components. Hence, total of the three dependent variables were used, including one measure of heart rate (Heart Rate Monitor Scale), state anxiety (The State Anxiety Scale of the State-Trait Anxiety Inventory for Children) and self rating scale of overt target behavioral symptoms of headaches, insomnia, and general tension. The sample consisted of 80 middle grade students who were randomly assigned to the four conditions. As expected there were no relationship between the measures of heart rate and state anxiety and the four groups were found to have equivalent pretest measures of heart rate and state anxiety. Two one way ANCOVA designs were employed to compare the four treatment groups on post-test anxiety score and heart-beat measures. Non-parametric post-test designs (Kruskall Wallis Test) was used to $ compare the rating of the target behavioral symptoms of headaches, insomnia and general tension. The findings of this study can be summarized as PRT and YM techniques are more effective rather than CAT and MAG strategies. Yoga meditation proved more effective to reduce heart rate than PRT and MAG strategies. PRT and Yoga meditation reduce headaches and general tension. CAT is more effective to relax headaches then the MAG techniques.

Edwards (1987) conducted a research on the long term effects of Sidha yoga such as meditation, chanting, seva, japa and pooja on psychological change and spiritual growth of the selected subjects. The people who had been practicing yoga for ten or more years were chosen as subjects. 13 infants were divided into three sub groups. The first group involved four (4) in formats and called ashramites. Second was of four (4) in formats and called swamis and the third had five (5) in number and participated in the series of 3 in- depth interviews based on Spradlay's method and completed a written validation procedure. They were authorised to add, or correct the researcher's conclusion regarding their experience of Sidha yoga. Post-research results clarified that the practice of Sidha yoga brings physical, mental, emotional, conceptual, relational and attitudinal changes for long term. It has its long term effects on purifying the body, heart and mind. It increases one's Shakti and the person becomes more conscious and expands one's experience of unconditional love. It also positively affects the relationship of guru-discipline and also helps to awaken the Kundilini.

Digamber (1985) states that the primary aim of asana and Pranayama is to develop the inherent capabilities of an individual and thus make his life fuller, richer, and more efficient. He further describe that these yogic practices totally change the mental attitudes and indicate virtues like honesty, sincerity and self actualization that contribute to health, happiness and harmony in life.

Bernhard (1980) conducted a double blind study to see the effect of Transcendental meditation on concentration ability. Practitioners of transcendental meditation were randomly assigned to two treatment group. One group mediated for 20 minutes while the other read a test quietly. The test d2 (Briehkenkamp 1962) was used and both the groups were tested before and after the treatment to measure their concentration ability. After initial medical checkup all the participants (N = 27, boys = 14, girls = 13, age = 15 to 63 yrs) were tested for anxiety and personality variables. Yogic intervention (Shavasana – meditation) revealed significant reduction in anxiety and improvement in overall personality. The result indicates that savasana – meditation produced emotional stability and physical relaxation significantly.

Vinod et al. (1984) carried out a study on an adolescent group of 14 boys and 13 girls to investigate the effects of yogic practices on anxiety, neuroticism and extraversion. Treatment of 10 Asana, 2 Pranayama and 3 Kriyas were given to them. Data was collected by Sinha's Anxiety Scale and Modestly Personality Inventory. The analysis of data on pre-test and post-test scores exhibited a significant fall in mean values on anxiety as well as neuroticism. They concluded that yogic practices produce a significant decrease in anxiety, neuroticism and general hostility. Their study further revealed that yogic practices have positive effect on physical relaxation and decrease in emotional disturbances.

Kochar (1976) studied the ―Influence of Yogic Practices on Mental Fatiguell His sample comprised 38 young boy in the age group 14 - 18. His treatment schedule consisted of 8 asana and 2 Pranayama exercises. Shavasana was prolonged for 5 to 8 minutes after the session. The yogic training continued for six months. He found that all the 38 subjects exhibited a significant positive effect of yogic practices in reducing mental fatigue, postponing the onset of fatigue and a significant improvement in performance on mental work.

Stephen (1974) conducted an experiment on the effects of yoga therapy on conflict resolution, self-concept and emotional adjustment. He used yoga therapy as psychotherapeutic tool to further examine the psychotherapeutic effectiveness of yoga, transcendental meditation and the like. A stratified random assignment of subjects to groups and random assignment of groups to experimental and control conditions were performed. Measures of conflict resolution, self concept and emotional adjustment were the dependent variables which had hypothesized relationship to the independent variables. The Conflicts Resolution Inventory and the Tennessee Self Concept Scale were scored and the results were transferred to punched cards for computer analysis. For significant differences 'f test' was used between experimental and control groups. The result indicated that yoga therapy is an effective method of stimulating positive change in term of conflict resolution between actual and desired behaviors, feelings of the sense of self-esteem, identity, self-satisfaction perception of own behavior, physical self, moral-ethical self, personal self as well as defensiveness and emotional adjustment.

Deshmukh (1971) worked upon yoga in management of psychoneurotic, psychotic and psychomatic conditions. 106 Patients, attending the yoga institute Santacruz, were selected for the study. Each patient was firstly interviewed by the psychiatrist and also examined by the physician when it was necessary for them. The patient was also subjected to pathological, radiological and electro cardiographic examination whenever indicated. At the end of 6 weeks each patient was again tested. From the data presented, it appeared that there was a high rate of improvement among patients.

Chapter III

METHODOLOGY

The 3rd chapter methodology deals with the procedure followed towards the selection of subjects, experimental design and procedure, dependent variables, selection of variables, instrument reliability, orientation of the subject, yogic training schedule, collection of data and statistical analysis have been explained.

Selection of Subjects

Sixty male subjects were selected at a simple random sampling technique, from Brilliant Public School, Aligarh which is located in district Aligarh Uttar Pradesh India. The subjects were dividing into two groups of 30 each. 30 male subjects were assigned as the experimental group and another 30 subjects were assigned as the control group during the academic year 2017-2018.

They were the student's ages ranged from 14 to 17 years. All the subjects were assembled in a lawn/covered area to act as subjects. The researcher explained to them the importance, purpose and nature of the experiment and the process to be used to collect their Psychological and Anthropometry data. Nextly the roles of the students for the duration of the experimentation were also explained in detail. Investigator requested to subjects to co-operate and participate actively alike.

Selection of variables

For this study, the researcher pool of scientific literature related to the different yogic practices was reviewed on selected variables from online research database, research papers, books and journals. Taking into thought the availability of the instrument, feasibility criteria and the relevance of the variables of the present study in consultation with subject experts, teachers and supervisor the following variables were selected.

Dependent Variables

1. Height
2. Kinesthetic sense
3. Memory (L.T.M.)
4. Creativity

Independent variable

Yogic practices (Suryanamaskar, Asanas, Pranayamas, Kriya and Yoga Nidra)

Criterion measures for dependent variables

1. Height was measured by Stadiometer.

2. Kinesthetic sense was measured by Arm Raising Test.

3. Memory was measured by B.B. Asthana Memory Test.

4. Creativity was measured by Passi test of Creativity.

Instrument reliability

Instruments like stadiometer, metronome and stopwatch were manufactured by standard companies and standard instruments were used, thus their calibrations were reliable to be accepted for the purpose of the study. Instruments reliability was checked also by the test-retest method.

Reliability of Data

The reliability of data was ensured by establishing the instrument accuracy and reliability of subjects.

Reliability of subjects

The subject's reliability was ensured by guaranteeing the subjects that their responses were kept confidential and were used only for research purposes. The subjects were requested to express frankly and freely as per the instruction contained in each instrument. This naturally had a salutary effect on their results that their bias in responding to the statement/questions contained in the various instruments was minimized and reliability of data-enhanced considerably.

Orientation of the Subjects

The researcher was present together with the subjects of the experimental and control groups throughout the experimentation of both pre-test and post-data. The testing procedure for conducting the tests and the technique and tools of scoring was particularly explained as well as demonstrated by the researcher to improve in quality of the tester's consistency.

Test Administration Procedures

Procedure of test

The experiment was conducted 5 days a week for a period of three months (excluding the period of collecting the data) in the morning.

HEIGHT MEASURMENT

Equipment: -Stadiometer

Method: - The subject was asked to stand on stadiometer platform barefooted with back against the wall/pole and feet together. While subject was asked to stretch the body upwards as much as possible with his heels sticking to the ground. Tuck in your chin and look straight ahead. The researcher adjusts the horizontal arm on the stadiometer so that it was resting on the top of the subjects head.

Scoring: - The measurement of standing height was recorded in cm.

KINESTHETIC SENSE

Equipment: - Arm Raising Test

Method: - Performer stands facing away from Arm Angle Chart, which was positioned on the wall. The chart was adjusted to shoulder height. Performer was asked to raise their shoulder at $45^{O.}$ He was blindfolded and given three trials to attempt to repeat the 45° movement by raising fully extended arm that is pronated so chart may be easily read. Positive or negative deviations in degree are recorded.

Scoring: - Test score was total deviations in degree regardless of signs for each angle divided by number of trials.

MEMORY

Equipment: - Dr. B.B. Asthana Memory Test

Method: - After satisfying that the subject has followed and understood the task, the actual experiment was started. Each pair was presented for two seconds, with the help of a memory drum (or showing cards for 2 seconds with the help of a stopwatch). The researcher showed a pair of words after giving a ready signal. Immediately after showing the stimulus pair researcher speaks the number one, two, three and four; according to the sequence giving in the sheet. The subject repeats the pair according to the number given to them. Now the researcher speaks another number and the subject starts writing backward according to instructions given before starting the test. The researcher starts to stopwatch simultaneously and the tasks continue for 2 min. The researcher now asks the subject to stop. The subject on hearing 'Stop' speaks the pair of words presented to them, which were noted down by 'researcher' on the datasheet. The same procedure was followed for all the pairs of words.

The responses of the subject were noted down on the data sheet.

Sr. No.	Stimulus Words	Times to be repeated	Number string	Response
1.	QUEEN- PONY	1	87	
2.	FRUIT- SOLDIER	2	67	
3.	BUS - COW	4	97	
4.	SHIRT -JEEP	3	55	
5.	RAT- CAP	2	56	
6.	SWORD - TREE	4	77	
7.	DOG - CAR	3	98	
8.	FROCK - HEN	1	86	
9.	BALOON - FLOWER	4	84	
10.	GEM - FAN	3	44	
11.	LION - SHEEP	1	48	
12.	BAT - COAT	2	53	
13.	PEN - CAT	3	56	
14.	DEAR - BOAT	1	89	
15.	BADGE - SHEEP	2	98	
16.	HAT- FOX	4	65	

The responses should be tabulated accordingly. Then find out the correct score for all the four retention intervals.

CREATIVITY

Equipment: - Passi Test of Creativity

 Method: - Six tests include in "The Passi Test of creativity", namely

  i. The Seeing Problem Test,

ii.   The Unusual Uses Test

iii.   The Consequences Test

iv.   The Test of Inquisitiveness

v.   The Square Puzzle Test and

vi.   The Blocks Test of Creativity.

The first three tests were verbal in nature. The last three tests can be classified as partially non-verbal because the test materials of these three tests present the non-verbal type of stimuli. The first four tests can be administered individually as well as in convenient groups of nearly thirty subjects at a time. The fifth test of Square Puzzle can either be administered individually or in groups not exceeding six students per administration. The sixth test, namely the Blocks test of Creativity can be administered individually.

i.   **The Seeing Problems Test** – In the case of the seeing problems test, each accepted response was given a credit of one score representing seeing problem (SP). The total number of such accepted responses on the whole test consisting of all the four items represents the score of the Seeing Problems(SP)

ii.   **The Unusual Uses Test** – The most common responses were considered to be the least original and as such, given a weightage of zero, whereas the least common responses were given a maximum credit of four. The sum of such weightage scores is taken to be the score on originality (UO). The summed scores of fluency (UF), flexibility (UX) and originality (UO) yielded an estimate of creativity (UC) as measured by the Unusual Uses Test.

iii.   **The Consequences Test** – The test was designed to measure the dimension of fluency (CF) and originality (CO). Fluency (CF) was represented by the sum total of accepted responses on the test. The score of originality (CO) was represented by the total number of indirect or remote responses. The summated scores of fluency (CF) and originality (CO) represents a score of creativity (CC) as measured by the Consequences Test.

iv.   **The Test of Inquisitiveness** – In this test, the relevant and mutually exclusive question asked about the metronome and about the playing card displaying the sentence "A FEW CHILDREN CANNOT TOUCH IT" was counted in order to get the score of Inquisitiveness (INQ). The relevant and mutually exclusive questions asked were given in the scoring manual. Valid questions get 1 mark and valid question but repeated questions get zero marks. Sum up of the marks were the score of Test of Inquisitiveness.

v.   **The Square Puzzle Test** – This test was intended to measure the dimensions of persistency (PER). The score of a student on persistency (PER) was derived from the time taken by him on the task. The total score on persistency (PER) was equal to the number of completed minutes on the task after deducting three minutes given to the subjects for initial practice and familiarity with the test material.

vi.   **The Blocks Test of Creativity** – The dimensions of fluency (BF), flexibility (BX) and originality (BO) are measured with the help of the Blocks Test of Creativity. The most frequently occurring responses was considered to the least original and was given a weightage of zero and the least occurring responses was considered to be the most original and was assigned a weightage of four on a five point scale. The sum total of these weights yields the score of originality (BO). Creativity score (BC) on this test was the summation of the scores on the dimensions of fluency (BF), Flexibility (BX) And Originality (BO).

Yogic Training programme

In this study, the researcher considered two groups experimental group and control group. It was decided that the training will be provided for the experimental group and not for the control group. As per the opinion of yoga experts, opinion of the supervisor and going through literature finally we have decided that suryanamaskar and selected asanas, pranayamas, kriya and yoga nidra for the development of height, kinesthetic sense, memory and creativity had been selected before the commencement of actual training. The training was given continuously for 3 months, 5 days a week. The training schedule was from 6:30 to 7:45 morning (excluding pre and post-data collection). During the training session, the yogic practices group was instructed to perform selected yogic practices for a specific time which was determined by the researcher as per schedule however control group did not participate in any specific training but they perform regular physical activities. The training program was executed in the morning under the supervision of the researcher who himself had an adequate level of training and knowledge of yogic practices. The entire activity was assisted and helped by the physical education teachers who were properly trained.

Yogic practice schedule for three months

Serial No.	Name of the Activity	1st Month (Time in minutes)	2nd Month (Time in minutes)	3rd Month (Time in minutes)
1.	Suryanamaskar	4	4	4
2.	Ardhachandrasana	2	3	4
3.	Vrikshasana	2	3	4
4.	Tadasana	2	3	4
5.	SuptaVajrasana	2	3	4
6.	Vakrasana	2	3	4
7.	Paschimottanasana	2	3	4
8.	Dhanurasana	2	3	4
9.	Sarvangasana	2	3	4
10.	Halasana	2	3	4
11.	Chakrasana	2	3	4
12.	Kapalbhati	2	3	3
13.	Anulom –vilom pranayama	4	4	4
14.	Bhramari pranayama	4	4	4
15.	Om chanting	4	4	4
16.	Yoga nidra	5	5	5

(Shavasana and Makarasana) relaxation asanas were performed in supine and prone position after each asana to bringing in normal state.

Suryanamaskar

Ardhachandrasana

Vrikshasana

Tadasana

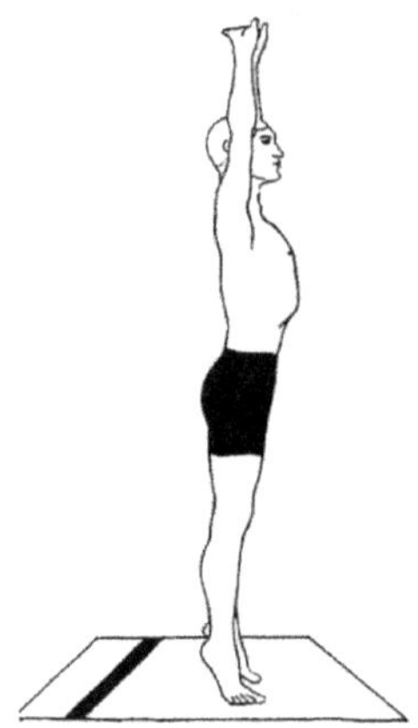

Supta Vajrasana

Vakrasana

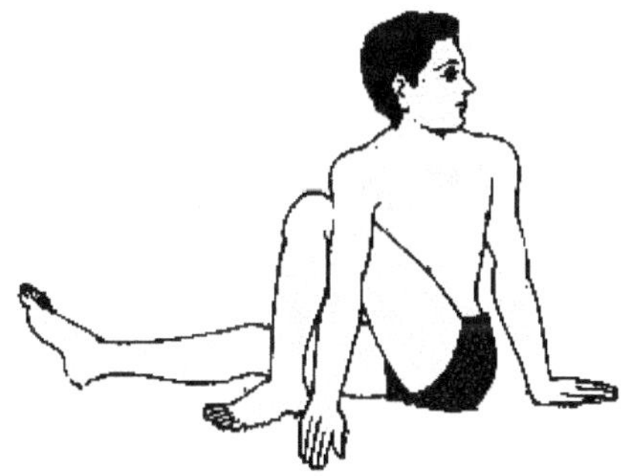

Paschimottanasana

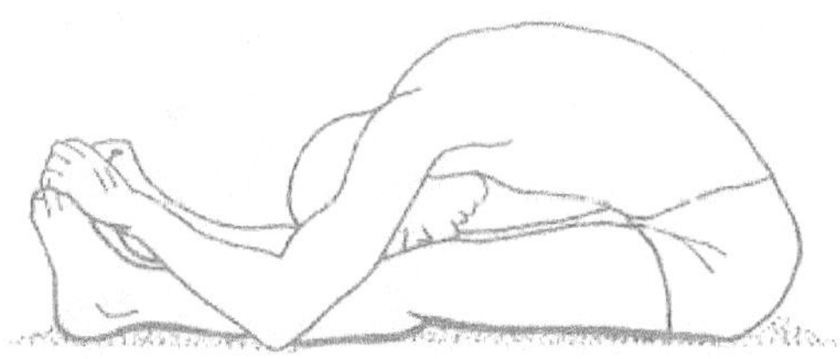

Dhanurasana

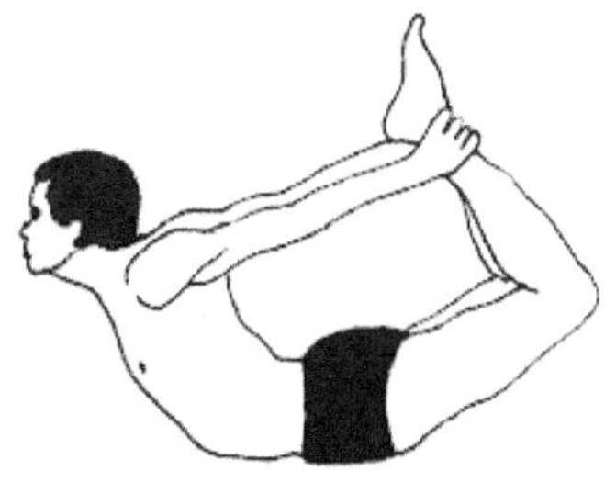

Sarvangasana

Halasana

Chakrasana

Kapalbhati

Anulom –vilom pranayama

Bhramari pranayama

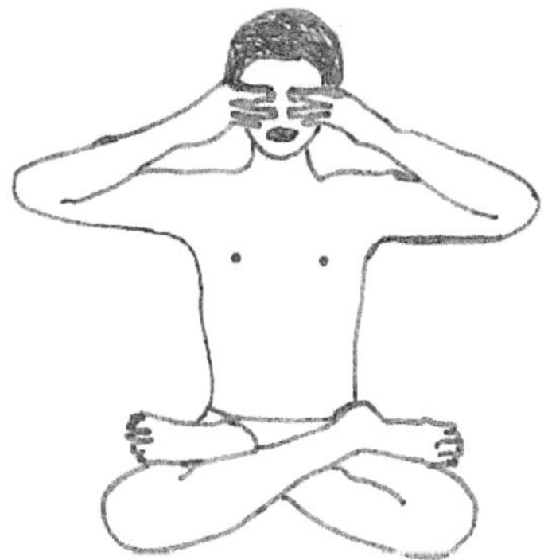

Shavasana

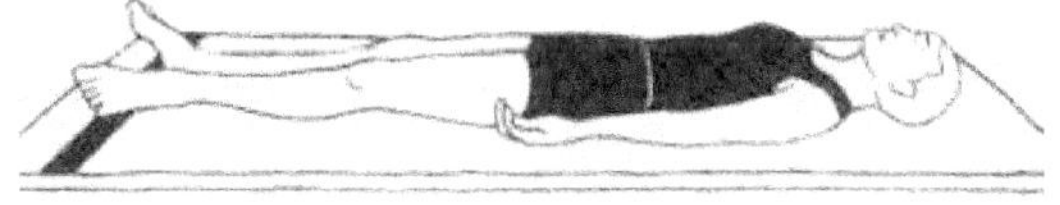

Makarasana

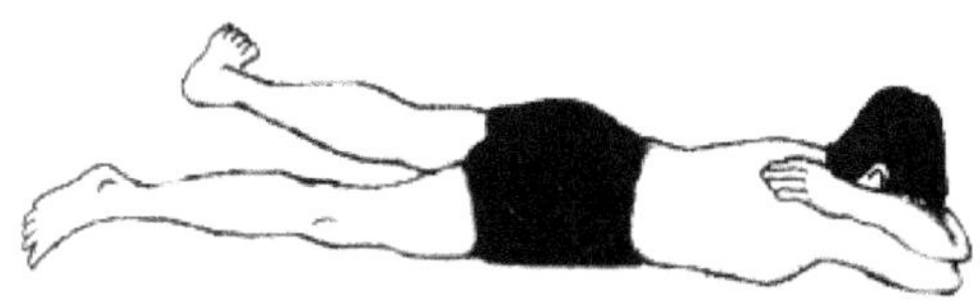

Collection of Data

Ratings and responses for all 60 subjects collected by the researcher before as well as after the training were scored and then entered into the SPSS software.

Statistical Analysis

A paired sample T-Test was applied to evaluate this study of yogic practices on height, kinesthetic sense, memory and creativity among school going children. The level of significance was chosen at 0.05.

Chapter IV

ANALYSIS OF DATA AND DISCUSSION OF FINDINGS

In the 4th chapter analysis of data and discussion of findings has been done. This study was conducted with the aim to derive the effect of selected yogic practices on Height, Kinesthetic sense, Memory and Creativity. To assess Height, Stadiometer was used, Arm Raising Test was used to assess Kinesthetic Sense, B.B. Asthana Memory Test was used to assess Memory, Passi Test of Creativity was used to assess Creativity. Therefore, the difference between the initial scores of the experimental and control group at pre-tests had to be taken into consideration during the analyses of the post-test difference between the final scores. This was achieved by using a t-test.

The paired sample T-Test was used to determining the differences if any among the pre and post-test means for the data pertaining to the variables in this study. For all the cases the level of significance was fixed at a 0.05 level of confidence. Before running the t-test it was very important to check that our data was normally distributed.

Table:1 Comparison of Mean between pre and post-test of Control Group of Height								
	Mean	N	Std. Deviation	Std. Error Mean	Mean Difference	t	df	p
Pre	167.35	30	6.56	1.20	.24	3.87	29	.001
Post	167.59	30	6.50	1.19				

Interpretation: Results of the table 1 exhibit that the control group (t =3.87,p = 0.001, p < 0.05) showed statistically significant mean differences (0.24) exist between pre-test and post-test. It is due to the age group of (14-17 years) Height increases normally so that statistical analysis shows a significant difference.

<table>
<tr><td colspan="10">Table:2 Comparison of Mean between pre and post-test of Experimental Group of Height</td></tr>
<tr><td></td><td>Mean</td><td>N</td><td>Std. Deviation</td><td>Std. Error Mean</td><td>Mean Difference</td><td>t</td><td>df</td><td>p</td></tr>
<tr><td>Pre</td><td>165.89</td><td>30</td><td>6.55</td><td>1.20</td><td rowspan="2">1.19</td><td rowspan="2">15.50</td><td rowspan="2">29</td><td rowspan="2">.000</td></tr>
<tr><td>Post</td><td>167.08</td><td>30</td><td>6.66</td><td>1.22</td></tr>
</table>

Interpretation: Results of the table 2 exhibit that the experimental group (t =15.50, p = 0.000, p < 0.05) showed statistically significant mean differences (1.19) exist between pre-test and post-test. The results of the aforementioned study indicate that there was a significant increase in Height due to the delivery of the yogic activity.

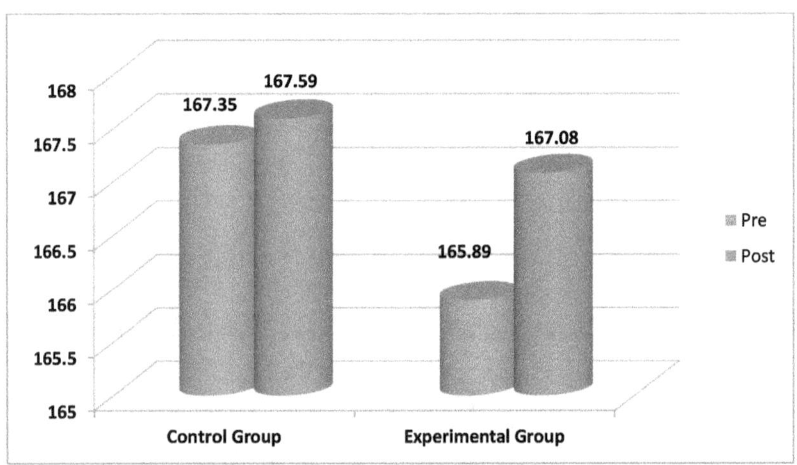

Figure 01 Graphical representation of Height Mean in Control and Experimental Group in Pre and Post-test.

<table>
<tr><td colspan="9">Table:3 Comparison of Mean between pre and post-test of Control Group of Kinesthetic Sense</td></tr>
<tr><td></td><td>Mean</td><td>N</td><td>Std. Deviation</td><td>Std. Error Mean</td><td>Mean Difference</td><td>t</td><td>df</td><td>p</td></tr>
<tr><td>Pre</td><td>5.76</td><td>30</td><td>2.42</td><td>.44</td><td rowspan="2">.19</td><td rowspan="2">1.37</td><td rowspan="2">29</td><td rowspan="2">.181</td></tr>
<tr><td>Post</td><td>5.57</td><td>30</td><td>2.34</td><td>.43</td></tr>
</table>

Interpretation: Results of the table 3 exhibit that the control group (t =1.37, p= 0.181, p > 0.05) showed statistically insignificant mean differences exist between pre-test and post-test. The results of the aforementioned study indicate that the absence of our yogic activity intervention does not cause any significant change in a kinesthetic sense among the subjects or it means that control subjects are unaffected in terms of kinesthetic sense.

Table:4 Comparison of Mean between pre and post-test of Experimental Group of Kinesthetic Sense								
	Mean	N	Std. Deviation	Std. Error Mean	Mean Difference	t	df	p
Pre	7.10	30	3.45	.63	3.92	6.82	29	.000
Post	3.18	30	1.88	.34				

Interpretation:

Results of the table 4 exhibit that the experimental group (t = 6.82, p = 0.000, p < 0.05) showed statistically significant mean differences exist between pre-test and post-test. The results of the aforementioned study indicate that there was a significant increase in Kinesthetic Sense due to the delivery of the yogic activity or it means that the experimental group enhances their Kinesthetic Sense.

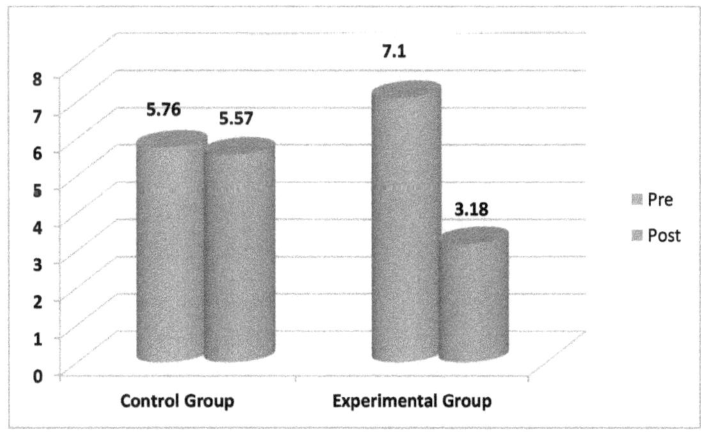

Figure 02 Graphical representation of Kinesthetic Sense Mean in Control and Experimental Group in Pre and Post-test.

Table: 5 Pre-Post Comparisons of Control and Experimental Group on Memory. (Repetition 1)

		Mean	N	Std. Deviation	Std. Error Mean	Mean Difference	t	df	p
Control group	Pre	1.40	30	.498	.091	.067	1.439	29	.161
	Post	1.47	30	.507	.093				
Experimental group	Pre	1.37	30	.490	.089	.700	8.226	29	.000
	post	2.07	30	.640	.117				

Interpretation: -

Results of the table 5 exhibit that the experimental group (t = 8.226,   p = 0.00, p < 0.05) showed statistically significant mean differences exist between pre-test and post-test and control group (t =1.439, p= 0.161, p > 0.05) explicated insignificant difference between pre-test and post-test. The results of the aforementioned study indicate that there was a significant increase in Memory (repetition 1) due to the delivery of the yogic activity.

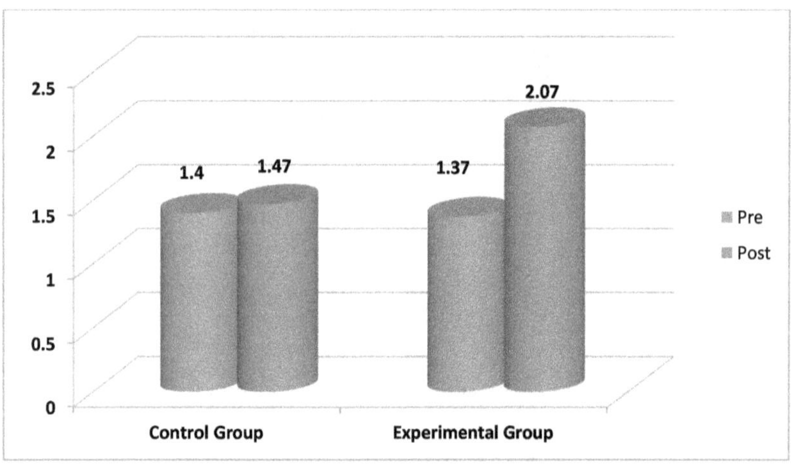

Figure 03 Graphical Representation of Memory Mean (Repetition 1) in Control and Experimental Group in Pre and Post-test.

<table>
<tr><td colspan="10">Table: 6 Pre-Post Comparisons of Control and Experimental Group on Memory.
(Repetition 2)</td></tr>
<tr><td></td><td></td><td>Mean</td><td>N</td><td>Std.
Deviation</td><td>Std. Error
Mean</td><td>Mean
Difference</td><td>t</td><td>df</td><td>p</td></tr>
<tr><td>Control group</td><td>Pre</td><td>1.43</td><td>30</td><td>.504</td><td>.092</td><td rowspan="2">.100</td><td rowspan="2">1.361</td><td rowspan="2">29</td><td rowspan="2">.184</td></tr>
<tr><td></td><td>Post</td><td>1.53</td><td>30</td><td>.571</td><td>.104</td></tr>
<tr><td>Experimental</td><td>Pre</td><td>1.33</td><td>30</td><td>.479</td><td>.088</td><td rowspan="2">1.033</td><td rowspan="2">11.547</td><td rowspan="2">29</td><td rowspan="2">.000</td></tr>
<tr><td>group</td><td>post</td><td>2.37</td><td>30</td><td>.556</td><td>.102</td></tr>
</table>

Interpretation:-

Results of the table 6 exhibit that the experimental group (t = 11.547,   p = 0.000, p < 0.05) showed statistically significant mean differences exist between pre-test and post-test and control group (t =1.361, p= 0.184, p > 0.05) explicated insignificant difference between pre-test and post-test. The results of the aforementioned study indicate that there was a significant increase in Memory (repetition 2) due to the delivery of the yogic activity.

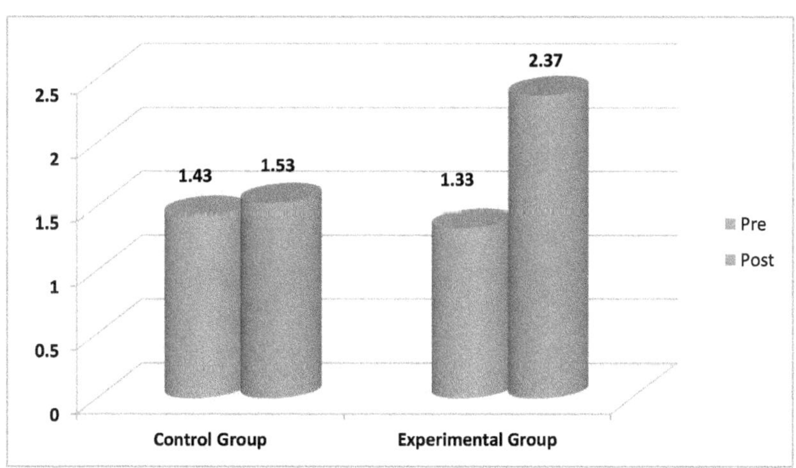

Figure 04 Graphical Representation of Memory Mean (Repetition 2) in Control and Experimental Group in Pre and Post-test.

Table: 7 Pre-Post Comparisons of Control and Experimental Group on Memory. (Repetition 3)									
		Mean	N	Std. Deviation	Std. Error Mean	Mean Difference	t	df	p
Control group	Pre	2.23	30	.626	.114	.200	1.989	29	.056
	Post	2.43	30	.568	.104				
Experimental group	Pre	2.13	30	.629	.115	.800	10.770	29	.000
	post	2.93	30	.583	.106				

Interpretation:-

Results of the table 7 exhibit that the experimental group (t = 10.770, p = 0.000, p < 0.05) showed statistically significant mean differences exist between pre-test and post-test and control group (t =1.989, p= 0.056, p > 0.05) explicated insignificant difference between pre-test and post-test. The results of the aforementioned study indicate that there was a significant increase in Memory (repetition 3) due to the delivery of the yogic activity.

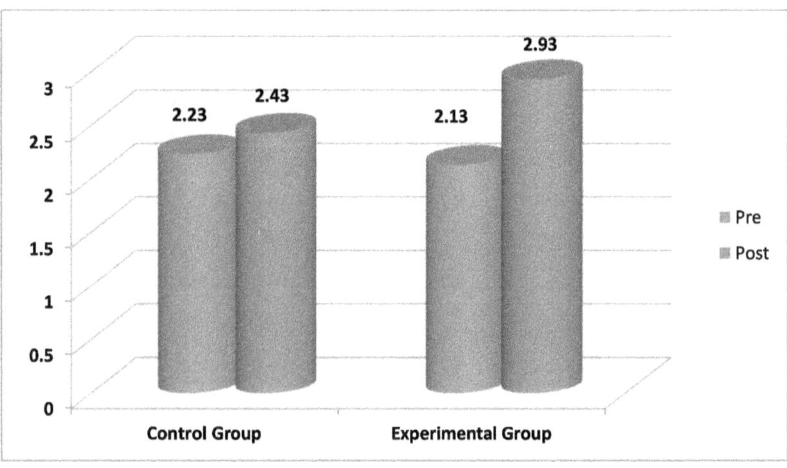

Figure 05 Graphical Representation of Memory Mean (Repetition 3) in Control and Experimental Group in Pre and Post-test.

Table: 8 Pre-Post Comparisons of Control and Experimental Group on Memory. (Repetition 4)									
		Mean	N	Std. Deviation	Std. Error Mean	Mean Difference	t	df	p
Control group	Pre	2.57	30	.728	.133	.100	1.795	29	.83
	Post	2.67	30	.711	.130				
Experimental group	Pre	2.33	30	.711	.130	1.233	9.280	29	.000
	post	3.57	30	.568	.104				

Interpretation:

Results of the table 8 exhibit that the experimental group (t = 9.280,   p = 0.000, p < 0.05) showed statistically significant mean differences exist between pre-test and post-test and control group (t =1.795, p= 0.83, p > 0.05) explicated insignificant difference between pre-test and post-test. The results of the aforementioned study indicate that there was a significant increase in Memory (repetition 4) due to the delivery of the yogic activity.

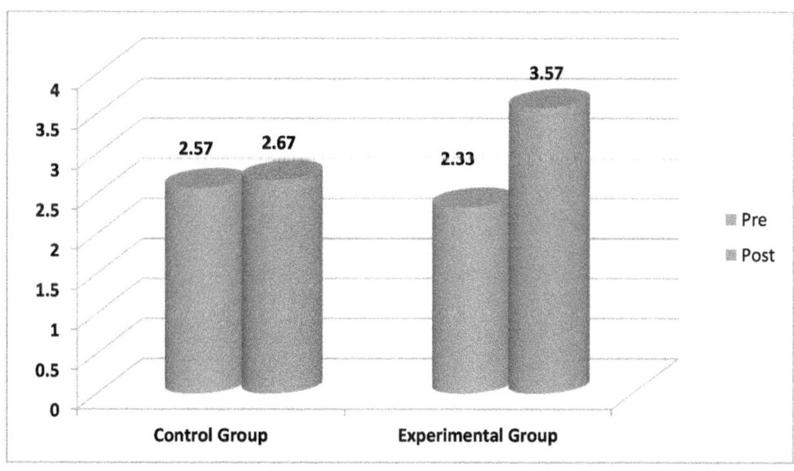

Figure 06 Graphical Representation of Memory Mean (Repetition 4) in Control and Experimental Group in Pre and Post-test.

<table>
<tr><td colspan="10">Table: 9 Pre-Post Comparisons of Control and Experimental Group on Creativity.
(The Seeing Problem Test)</td></tr>
<tr><td></td><td></td><td>Mean</td><td>N</td><td>Std.
Deviation</td><td>Std. Error
Mean</td><td>Mean
Difference</td><td>t</td><td>df</td><td>p</td></tr>
<tr><td>Control group</td><td>Pre</td><td>11.03</td><td>30</td><td>3.718</td><td>.679</td><td rowspan="2">.133</td><td rowspan="2">1.682</td><td rowspan="2">29</td><td rowspan="2">.103</td></tr>
<tr><td></td><td>Post</td><td>11.17</td><td>30</td><td>3.705</td><td>.677</td></tr>
<tr><td>Experimental</td><td>Pre</td><td>11.47</td><td>30</td><td>3.910</td><td>.714</td><td rowspan="2">6.033</td><td rowspan="2">16.455</td><td rowspan="2">29</td><td rowspan="2">.000</td></tr>
<tr><td>group</td><td>post</td><td>17.50</td><td>30</td><td>3.340</td><td>.610</td></tr>
</table>

Interpretation: -

Results of the table 9 exhibit that the experimental group (t = 16.455, p = 0.000, p < 0.05) showed statistically significant mean differences exist between pre-test and post-test and control group (t =1.682, p= 0.103, p > 0.05) explicated insignificant difference between pre-test and post-test. The results of the aforementioned study indicate that there was a significant increase in Creativity (The Seeing Problem Test) due to the delivery of the yogic activity.

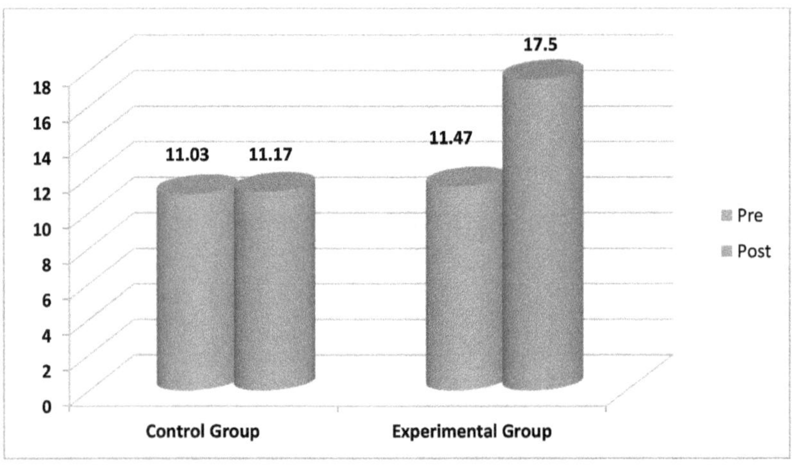

Figure 07 Graphical Representation of Creativity Mean (The Seeing Problem Test) in Control and Experimental Group in Pre and Post-test.

<table>
<tr><td colspan="10">Table: 10 Pre-Post Comparisons of Control and Experimental Group on Creativity.
(The Unusual Uses Test)</td></tr>
<tr><td></td><td></td><td>Mean</td><td>N</td><td>Std.
Deviation</td><td>Std. Error
Mean</td><td>Mean
Difference</td><td>t</td><td>df</td><td>p</td></tr>
<tr><td rowspan="2">Control group</td><td>Pre</td><td>20.67</td><td>30</td><td>11.232</td><td>2.051</td><td rowspan="2">.033</td><td rowspan="2">.083</td><td rowspan="2">29</td><td rowspan="2">.934</td></tr>
<tr><td>Post</td><td>20.70</td><td>30</td><td>9.639</td><td>1.760</td></tr>
<tr><td rowspan="2">Experimental
group</td><td>Pre</td><td>22.53</td><td>30</td><td>10.020</td><td>1.829</td><td rowspan="2">4.133</td><td rowspan="2">12.103</td><td rowspan="2">29</td><td rowspan="2">.000</td></tr>
<tr><td>post</td><td>26.67</td><td>30</td><td>8.942</td><td>1.633</td></tr>
</table>

Interpretation:-

Results of the table 10 exhibit that the experimental group (t = 12.103,   p = 0.000, p < 0.05) showed statistically significant mean differences exist between pre-test and post-test and control group (t =0.083, p= 0.934, p > 0.05) explicated insignificant difference between pre-test and post-test. The results of the aforementioned study indicate that there was a significant increase in Creativity (The Unusual Uses Test) due to the delivery of the yogic activity.

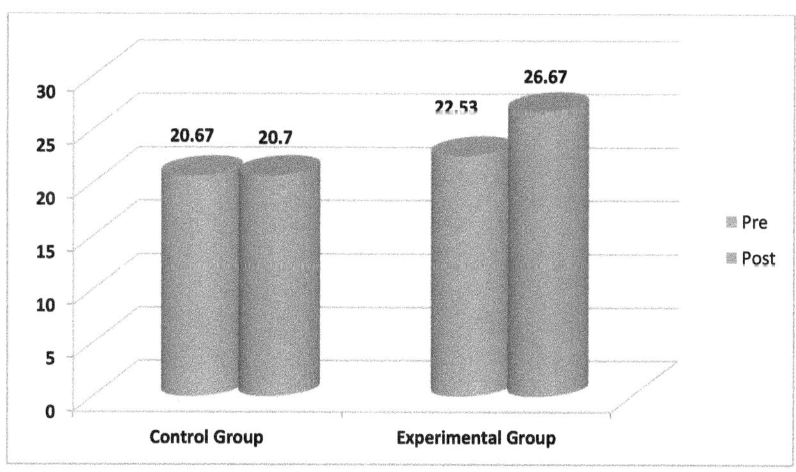

Figure 08 Graphical Representation of Creativity Mean (The Unusual Uses Test) in Control and Experimental Group in Pre and Post-test.

Table: 11 Pre-Post Comparisons of Control and Experimental Group on Creativity. (The Consequences Test)									
		Mean	N	Std. Deviation	Std. Error Mean	Mean Difference	t	df	p
Control group	Pre	8.87	30	3.340	.610	.033	.115	29	.909
	Post	8.90	30	2.631	.480				
Experimental group	Pre	9.77	30	4.264	.779	4.167	12.665	29	.000
	post	13.93	30	4.274	.780				

Interpretation-

Results of the table no.11 exhibit that the experimental group (t = 12.665, p = 0.000, p < 0.05) showed statistically significant mean differences exist between pre-test and post-test and control group (t =0.115, p= 0.909, p > 0.05) explicated insignificant difference between pre-test and post-test. The results of the aforementioned study indicate that there was a significant increase in Creativity (The Consequences Test) due to the delivery of the yogic activity.

.

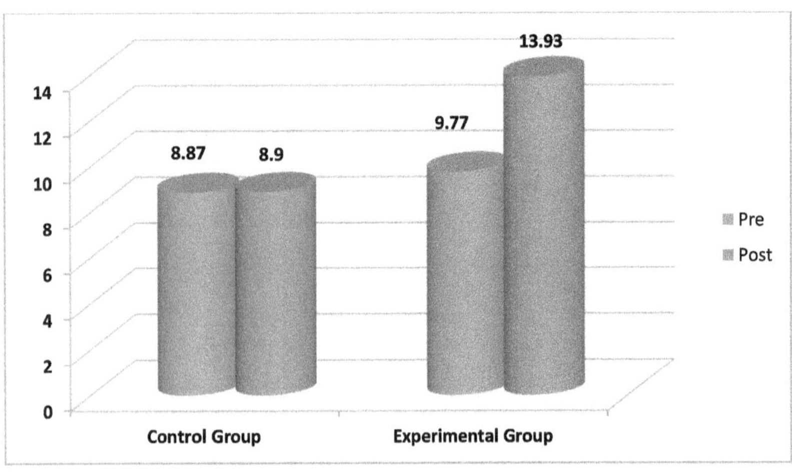

Figure 09 Graphical Representation of Creativity Mean (The Consequences Test) in Control and Experimental Group in Pre and Post-test.

		Mean	N	Std. Deviation	Std. Error Mean	Mean Difference	t	df	p
Control group	Pre	8.43	30	3.126	.571	.200	1.649	29	.110
	Post	8.63	30	2.871	.524				
Experimental group	Pre	8.83	30	3.075	.561	3.867	12.636	29	.000
	post	12.70	30	3.659	.668				

Interpretation:-

Results of the table no.12 exhibit that the experimental group (t = 12.636, p = 0.000, p < 0.05) showed statistically significant mean differences exist between pre-test and post-test and control group (t −1.649, p= 0.110, p > 0.05) explicated insignificant difference between pre-test and post-test. The results of the aforementioned study indicate that there was a significant increase in Creativity (The Test of Inquisitiveness) due to the delivery of the yogic activity.

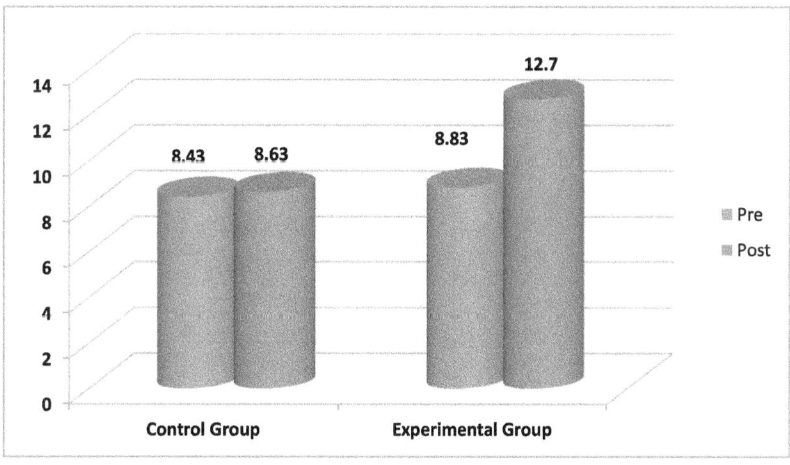

Figure 10 Graphical Representation of Creativity Mean (The Test of Inquisitiveness) in Control and Experimental Group in Pre and Post-test.

Table: 13 Pre-Post Comparisons of Control and Experimental Group on Creativity.									
(The Square Puzzle Test)									
		Mean	N	Std. Deviation	Std. Error Mean	Mean Difference	t	df	p
Control group	Pre	19.57	30	7.233	1.321	.333	1.262	29	.217
	Post	19.90	30	6.348	1.159				
Experimental group	Pre	19.27	30	7.825	1.429	2.833	9.334	29	.000
	post	22.10	30	7.752	1.415				

Interpretation:-

Results of the table no.13 exhibit that the experimental group (t = 9.334, p = 0.000, p < 0.05) showed statistically significant mean differences exist between pre-test and post-test and control group (t =1.262, p= 0.217, p > 0.05) explicated insignificant difference between pre-test and post-test. The results of the aforementioned study indicate that there was a significant increase in Creativity (The Square Puzzle Test) due to the delivery of the yogic activity.

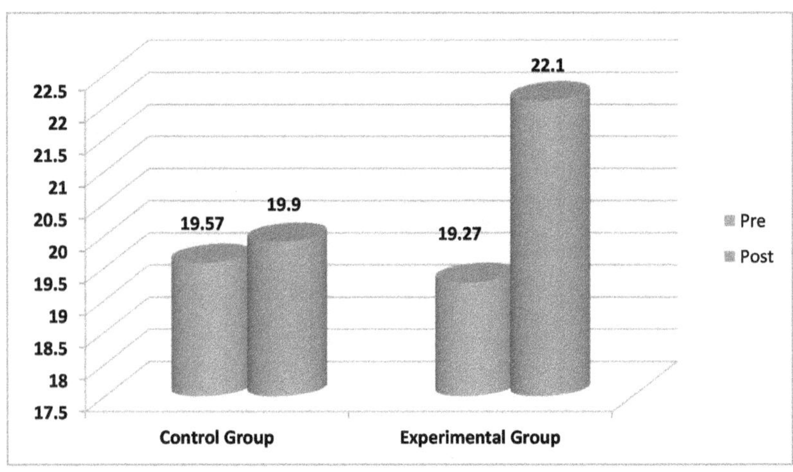

Figure 11 Graphical Representation of Creativity Mean (The Square Puzzle Test) in Control and Experimental Group in Pre and Post-test

Table: 14 Pre-Post Comparisons of Control and Experimental Group on Creativity.
(The Blocks Test of Creativity)

		Mean	N	Std. Deviation	Std. Error Mean	Mean Difference	t	df	p
Control group	Pre	34.73	30	12.476	2.278	.700	1.343	29	.190
	Post	35.43	30	11.377	2.077				
Experimental group	Pre	34.30	30	13.894	2.537	3.233	9.977	29	.000
	post	37.53	30	13.364	2.440				

Interpretation:-

Results of the table no.14 exhibit that the experimental group (t = 9.977, p = 0.000, p < 0.05) showed statistically significant mean differences exist between pre-test and post-test and control group (t =1.343, p= 0.190, p > 0.05) explicated insignificant difference between pre-test and post-test. The results of the aforementioned study indicate that there was a significant increase in Creativity (The Blocks Test of Creativity) due to the delivery of the yogic activity.

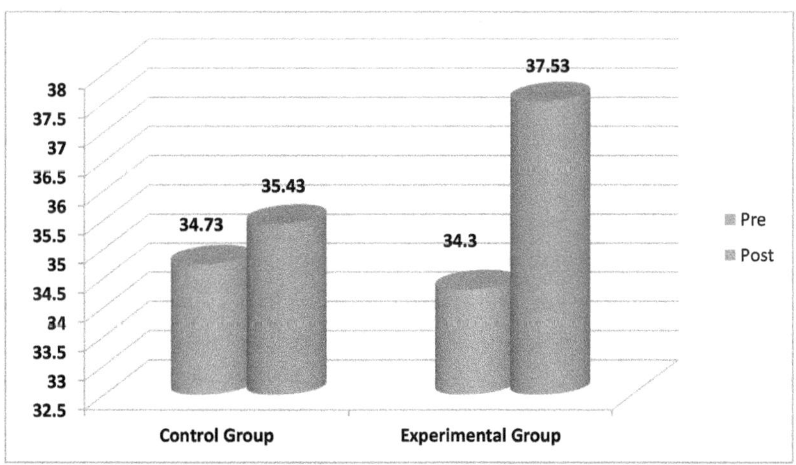

Figure 12 Graphical Representation of Creativity Mean (The Blocks Test of Creativity) in Control and Experimental Group in Pre and Post-test.

Discussion of Findings

This study was conducted to assess the effect of yogic practices on Height, Kinesthetic Sense, Memory and Creativity among school going male student's aged between 14-17 years. The data of analysis through paired sample t-test shows that the 12 weeks (3 months) yogic practices significantly improve in Height, Kinesthetic Sense, Memory and Creativity.

Height

Basically, asanas are expected to counteract psychosomatic disorder i.e. instability due to disturbances in muscle tonic rhythm on the human body. Tonic in balance in muscle can be removed with the practice of asana because they tackle the root causes of tonic imbalance like emotional stresses; anxiety etc. according to hath yoga, asanas contribute to stability, health and suppleness in the body. In asana practices, trunk movements are performed in all directions. The asanas keep the spine flexible and elastic or supple and prevent rigidity of its muscles and joints. These asanas can influence the growth and development of young children above 12 years of age. By stretching or producing traction on Vertebras and muscles the blood circulation around the joints is increased, so the nutritional value increases, and the waste products are efficiently removed. Thus, asanas bring a balance to the internal environment of the body which is known as homeostasis. It is an active process by which the constant hydrogen ion concentration, optimum supply of nutrients, removal of waste (toxic agent) products of metabolic process, etc. are balanced. Asanas and pranayamas keep thermoregulation i.e. body temperature constant at about 370 Celsius. High or low body temperature makes the body unable to work properly and hinders its natural growth. During yogic practices, more blood flows through the elementary system and oxygen through the respiratory system which eliminates maximum waste products that are gathered around different tissues through the excretory system. For this reason, the blood maintains a constant and balanced PH and hydrogen ion concentration in blood is maintained that is necessary because slight acetic blood changes the tonic rhythm of muscles and joint of vertebra column. For better health and tonic rhythm, blood pH is maintained at 7.4 slightly alkaline.

A most important factor that determines a child's height is the growth hormone GH or Somatotropin. The growth hormone is secreted by the anterior lobe of the pituitary gland. The pituitary gland is also known as hypophysis. It is located beneath the base of the brain, It secrets at least six different polypeptide hormone and influences the secretion of several other. Because of its widespread influence, the interior part of the pituitary gland was often called the "master gland". It is now known, however, that the hypothalamus actually controls anterior pituitary activity.

Thus hypothalamus should truly have the title "Master Gland". **Karagiorgos, A. et al. (1979)** Studies on exercise-induced production of GH have revealed a delay of a few minutes in GH secretion after exercise starts. **Galbo, H. (1983)** with successively increasing exercise levels, there is a sharp rise in GH production and total secretion. This would certainly be a beneficial response for muscles, bone and connective tissue growth, as well as for optimizing the metabolic mixture during exercise. The precise relationship between GH synthesis and exercise intensity and duration has not been established, nor has the stimulus been identified for increase GH production with exercise. Concurrent measurements of circulating lactate, alanine, pyruvate, blood glucose and body temperature reveal that none of these factors are responsible for regulating the pattern of GH secretion.

Growth hormone secretion during rest is influenced by a GH releasing factor that acts directly on the anterior pituitary gland. In fact, each of the primary pituitary hormones has its own hypothalamic releasing hormone, sometimes called a releasing factor. These releasing hormones are controlled by neural input to the hypothalamus by factors such as anxiety, stress and exercise.

Macintyre, J.G. (1987). The exact mechanism is not entirely clear by which GH and exercise interact to bring about increases in protein synthesis, cartilage formation, skeletal growth and cell proliferation. One hypothesis suggests that exercise directly simulates GH production and the pulsatile pattern of its release that in turn stimulates anabolic processes. It has been shown that exercise is directly associated with doubling of both GH pulse frequency and amplitude. Furthermore, exercise stimulates the production of endogenous opiates that facilitate GH rerelease by inhibiting the livers production of somatostatin, a hormone that blunts the release of GH. That is why we can say that the yogic practices have impact on height of an individual.

Our study is supported by **Lata Manju (2002); Raghav (2018); Datta (1993); Ganguly (2009); Shhell et al (1994).**

KINESTHETIC SENSE

The improvement of kinesthetic ability was due to the fact that yogic practices optimize the tonicity of muscles, tendon and joint as well as ear, eyes, skin (exteroceptors, interoceptors and proprioceptors) as they convey the information about the position, movement and balance of the body. These impulses are received, integrated and correlated in the brain below the level of consciousness (no activity of cortex) and appropriate motor impulses are passed on to the concerned muscles for action. It is clear that the central nervous system uses its lower center of integration for the maintenance of posture and equilibrium. These lower centers are situated in the medulla, pons, cerebellum, midbrain and basal ganglia. Various reflexes are integrated by their lower center below the level of consciousness to maintain the posture when asana is being performed with passive stretching. It also tranquilizes the mind and conditions it through the postural reflexes cerebellum - hypothalamus functional axis. The sympathetic activity is withdrawn and parasympathetic activity restores the stability on various levels. Now the body starts telling the mind through various sensations that are perceived from proprioceptors and are integrated by the lower center involuntarily. Secondly, there is a correlation between our mind and pranic activity like pranayama because our breathing is stopped for a few movements while threading the needle, which means if we try to control our breathing voluntarily, we would be able to control our mind. Because as long as breathing is continued and the air is moving in and out of the body, the mind remains unsteady. It means that for a steady mind we need to control our breathing. So we can say through yogic asana and pranayama activity kinesthetic ability can be improved. Our findings of this study are supported by **Singh (1996), Singh (2010), Kocher (1974), Pratap (1968), Ganguly and Gharote (1989).** Thus the result helps to conclude that the three months of yogic practices can be helpful to improve the kinesthetic ability of the subjects.

Memory

Long term memory gets significantly improved by the intervention of yogic practices. The improvement in memory was due to fact that yogic practices (Suryanamaskar, Asanas, Pranayamas, Kapalbhati Kriya and Yoga Nidra) tranquilize the body and mind by an absence of internal disturbances or overcome instability in body and mind. When asanas is performed with passive stretching then the muscles may surrender easily and muscle tone remains at its optimum level. We have seen that muscle tone is the basis of posture and gets influenced by the emotional or psychological state of an individual. Asana is counteracting instability due to disturbances (vikshepa) in the muscle tonic rhythm of the body. Asanas tackle the root causes of tonic imbalance like emotional conflicts, stresses, tension, depression, confidence level.

According to hath yoga, asanas contribute to stability, improve mental health and reduce insomnia (sleepness disorder). In asana, the sympathetic activity is withdrawn and parasympathetic activity restores the stability on various levels that is why the body starts telling the mind through various sensations that are perceived from the proprioceptor and are integrated by the lower center involuntarily. That is why a long-term effect of such performance is seen on the development of attention as well as concentration and the same line on the behavioral pattern (personality) of the individual.

Our findings are supported by **Sukla et al (2010); Kumar (2018); Lata, Manju (2002).** Secondly experimentally it has been found that attention, mental effort, different emotions and behavior pattern (tension and depression) bring about some modification in breathing. When we practice pranayama and make it rhythmic, it is possible to make our mind more balanced and to change the behavior pattern. Any activity which requires total concentration of our mind will also control our breath or which may be stopped for a while e.g. Air rifle shooting or threading the needle.

Chalevatechalechitenishchalenishchlambhavte

Yogi stahanutvama,tvamajyotitatovayumnirodhyte

(2nd chapter H.P.)

The body remains unsteady as long as breathing is continued and air moves in and out of the body, but the activity of the mind stops and becomes standstill when the breath is stopped or hold. By practicing pranayama, one can train and make himself/herself capable of attaining concentration and attention of the mind. Our findings are supported by **Singh (1996), Singh, Samay (2007).** Thus the result helps to conclude that the memory of an individual could be improved, his/her mind can be controlled and tranquilized by yogic practices.

Creativity

The evidence of yogic practices in children has positive effects mainly on psycho-physical, emotional intensity, self–awareness, self-confidence, stress reduction, behaviour and emotional maturity, memory performance and personality found significant improvement. **Michaelsen (2005), Telles (2000), Bussing et al. (2012), Kumar (2018).**

As we know that yoga means a connection of body, mind and soul. Through yoga, we can achieve physical, mental, social and spiritual health by practicing asana, pranayama, Yama and Niyamas. Asana is that which contributes to the stability and sense of well-being Sthira Sukham Asanam (Patanjali Yoga Sutra 2nd:46). Stability here does not mean the stability only of the posture but the stability of the body and mind as a whole. In nutshell, we can say that asana re-establish the harmonious functioning of the whole body and bring about an integration of the nervous system.

Experimentally it has been established that attention, mental effort, different emotions and behavioural pattern, bring about some modification in breathing. By pranayama, we regulate our breathing and make it rhythmic. It is possible to make our mind more balanced by practicing pranayama mind is trained and made capable of the process of Dhyan i.e. (concentration) of mind on one object or pointedness of mind is possible after long practice of pranayama. The research finding of **Hamid et al. (2014), Sandeep and Savita (2013)** research results show yogic activities support in minimizing stress and improve self-esteem, positive mental health, intellectual, attributes, physical appearance and self-concept in children.

Significant improvement in creativity is found due to fact that yogic practices bring to improve the harmonious functioning of the whole body and bring integration of the nervous system and significant improvement in personality. Yoga improves attention, concentration, intelligence, positive mental health, emotional maturity, self-confidence and stress reduction. Our findings are supported by **Pandya (2014).** So we can say that yogic practices are beneficial for improving creativity.

In the present study, it was found that the experimental group which was doing yogic practices was improved significantly their abilities in comparison to the control group. The analysis data received during the training programme of my subjects revealed that the experimental group showed significant improvement in the execution of concerning height, kinesthetic sense, memory and creativity of school going, children. Researcher, coaches, sports scientist always strives to search for the way and means to improve the performance and capacity of an individual. This study reinforces the effectiveness of the yogic training programme on height, kinesthetic sense, memory and creativity. So we can say that yogic practices are beneficial for the 14 -17 years age group.

Discussion of Hypothesis

It was hypothesized that yogic practices would not have any significant repercussions in height among school going children. The result shows that there exists a statistically significant difference in pre and post score of height of the subject. Therefore the first hypothesis was rejected because there was a positive effect of yogic practices on height.

It was hypothesized that yogic practices would not have any significant repercussions in kinesthetic sense among school going children. The result shows that there exists a statistically significant difference in pre and post score of kinesthetic sense of the subject. Therefore the second hypothesis was rejected because there was a positive effect of yogic practices on kinesthetic sense

It was hypothesized that yogic practices would not have any significant repercussions in memory among school going children. The result shows that there exists a statistically significant difference in pre and post score of memory of the subject. Therefore the third hypothesis was rejected because there was a positive effect of yogic practices on memory.

It was hypothesized that yogic practices would not have any significant repercussions in creativity among school going children. The result shows that there exists a statistically significant difference in pre and post score of creativity of the subject. Therefore the third hypothesis was rejected because there was a positive effect of yogic practices on creativity.

REFERENCES

Albert, R. S.; Runco, M. A. (1999), 'A history of research on creativity', In Sternberg, R. J. Handbook of Creativity. (Cambridge University Press) p. 5-6.

Annakili, C.M. (1993). A Comparative Study of Yoga Asana and Gymnastic In Selected Physical, Physiological and Psychological Variables. Unpublished M.Phil thesis, Alagappa University, India.

Avalle, A. Shalabg and Vallumurgan, V,(2008) "Effect of Selected Yogic Exercise and Psychological Skill Training on Selected Psycho Physiological and Psychomotor Variables of High- Level Participants", Yoga Mimamsa, XLI.1.

Barnes,B.L. and Nagarkar, S.(1989) Yoga Education and Scholastic Achievement. India Journal of clinical Psychology.16(2): 96-98

Beam, J.C. (1955). Serial learning and conditioning under real life stress.J. Abnorm. Soc. Psychol., 51,543-551.

Berger, Bonnie, G. and Owen, David R. (1988). "Stress Reduction and Mental Enhancement in Four Exercise Modes ", Swimming Body Conditioning, Hatha Yoga and Fencing, Research Quarterly, 60: PP.148-159.

Bern hard A. Sobel, (1980) "Transcendental Meditation and Concentration Ability", Perceptual & Motor Skills, 50, 779 – 802.

Bhomik Sanjib and Pant Gaurav (2010) "Effect of Yogic Exercises on Selected Psychomotor Variables in Physically Challenged Students", Yoga Mimamsa, Vol. XLI, No. 4, 347.

Bilderbeck, A. C., Farias, M., Brazil, I. A., Jakobowitz, S., & Wikholm, C. (2013). Participation in a 10-week course of yoga improves behavioural control and decreases psychological distress in a prison population. *Journal of psychiatric research, 47*(10), 1438-1445.

Brown RP, and Gerbarg PL.et.al (2005). "Sudarshan Kriya Yogic Breathing in the Treatment of Stress, Anxiety, And Depression. Part II--Clinical Applications And Guidelines." J Altern Complement Med.11 (4):PP. 711-7.

Bussing, A., Michalsen, A., Khalsa, S. B. S., Telles, S., & Sherman, K. J. (2012). Effects of yoga on mental and physical health: a short summary of reviews. *Evidence-Based Complementary and Alternative Medicine, 2012*.

Byrne, A., & Byrne, D. (1993). The effect of exercise on depression, anxiety and other mood states: a review. *Journal of psychosomatic research, 37*(6), 565-574.

Chidambara Raja S. (2010) "Effect of yogic practice and physical fitness on flexibility, anxiety and blood pressure" Indian journal for research in physical education and sports sciences, vol. 1

D. Sakthignanavel, (1995) "Effect of continuous running, yogic pranayama, and combination of continuous running and yogic pranayama exercise on cardio-respiratory endurance, selected physiological and psychological variables" *Unpublished doctoral dissertation*, Annamalai University,.

D.K. Deshmukh, (1971). "Yoga in Management of Psyneurotic Psychotic and Psychosonatic Condition", Journal of the Yoga Institute, XXI

Dalal, Geeta (2002): "Positive Health through Yoga." Paper Presented in The International Conference on "Yoga Research and Value Education", Held at Kaivalya Dhama, Lonavla (India), 28-31.

Datta, Uma (1993) Comparative effect of yoga and gymnastic programmes on growth pattern of primary school children. Ph.D. Thesis Jiwaji university, Gwalior.

Desai, J. and Ram J. (1979). Effect of asana on skill development in basketball (unpublished master thesis). Jiwaji University, Gwalior.

Digamber, S. (1985); Abstracts and Proceeding of Conference on Yoga and Science held at Kaivalayedhama; Lonavala, India, p. 139-145.

Edwards, Lawrence Roger (1987).Psychological Change and Spiritual Growth through the Practice of Siddha Yoga. Dissertation Abstracts International.48/02, p. 340-A.

Freeman, G.L. (1933). Facilitative and inhibitory effects of muscular tension upon performance. Amer. Journal of psychology, 45, 17-52

Galbo, H. (1983) Hormonal and Metabolic Adaptation to Exercise. New York, G.T. Verlag.

Ganguly, S.K. (2009), "Yogic practices for holistic health and fitness", Vyayam Vidnyan, Vol.42, No.3, p. 23.

Ganguly, S.K. and Gharote, M.L. (1989). Effect of Yogic training on endurance and flexibility. Yoga Mimamsa,27. 3 and 4, 29-39.

Gharote M.L. (1987). "Effect of every day and alternate day Yoga training of physical fitness of school children Ayurveda and yoga, 7, 9-5.

Hamid Dehghanfara, Maryam Alicheshmealaeeb, Mahvash Noorbakhsha (2014) "The Effect of Yoga Training on Stress and Self Esteem and It's Relation To Emotional Intelligence" Journal of Research in Applied sciences. Vol., 1(5): 109-112,

Hegde, K.S. (1983). Effect of yogic asanas and physical exercise on body flexibility in middle aged men. The Yoga review, summer and autumn, 3(2&3):75-79.

Indirani, L (1993) Effects of Yogasanas on selected physical, physiological and psychological variables among school boys. Unpublished master of philosophy theses, Physical Education Department Alagappa University.

J. West et.al. (2004), "Effects of Hatha Yoga and African Dance on Perceived Stress, Affect, and Salivary Cortisol", Annals of Behavioral Medicine, 28: 2, p. 114-118.

James A. and Raub M.S., (2002), "Psychophysiologic Effects of Hatha Yoga on Musculoskeletal and Cardiopulmonary Function: A Literature Review", The Journal of Alternative and Complementary Medicine, 8(6), 797-812.

Janowiak, J. J. (1993). Theoretical Foundations of Yoga Meditation: A Contribution to Self-Actualization and Stress Management.

Kalayil, John A. (1988). A Controlled Comparison of Progressive Relaxation and Yoga Meditation as Method to Relieve Stress in Middle Grade School Children. Dissertation abstracts International. 49/1, p. 100A.

Karagiorgos, A., et al.(1979). Growth hormone response to continuous and intermittent exercise.Med.Sci.Sports,11:302.

Kloubec, J. A. (2010). "Pilates Improvement of Muscle Endurance, Flexibility, Balance, and Posture". Journal of Strength and Conditioning Research, Volume: 24, Issue-3, pp. 661-667.

Kocher, H.C. (1974), Some appraisal of steadiness and two hand co-ordination as result of yogic practices. Yoga Mimamsa, Vol. XXI 384, 131-148.

Kochar, H.C. (1976), Influence of Yogic Practices on Mental Fatigue. Yoga Mimansa, 28 (2); 3.

Kumar, Durvesh (2018).Effects of selected yogic practices on Psycho-physiological variables on male students. Ph.D. Thesis Aligarh Muslim University.

Kumar, Praveena, et. al., (2011), "Effect of Yogic Pranayama and Meditation on Selected Physical and Physiological Variables", Asian Journal of Physical Education and Computer Science in Sports, 4(1): 74-76.

Lata, Manju (2002) Comparative effect of aerobic exercises and selected yogic practices on the psychosomatic disorders. Ph.D. Thesis, Aligarh Muslim University, Aligarh.

Macintyre, J.G. (1987). Growth hormone and athletes. Sports Med., 4:129.

Mahalinggam, L. (2014). Effects of meditation techniques on selected psychological variables of attention and concentration in women volleyball players. International journal of resent research and applied studies. Vol. 1 (5):62-65.

Michalsen, A., Grossman, P., Acil, A., Langhorst, J., Ludtke, R., Esch, T., Dobos, G.(2005). Rapid stress reduction and anxiolysis among distressed women as a consequence of a three-month intensive yoga programme. Medical science monitor, 11(12), CR555-CR561.

Mitchell, J. T., Zylowska, L., & Kollins, S. H. (2015). Mindfulness meditation training for attention-deficit/hyperactivity disorder in adulthood: current empirical support, treatment overview, and future directions. *Cognitive and behavioral practice, 22*(2), 172-191.

Muthukumar, L.   (2007) "The Effect of Yogic Practices on the Development of Physical Fitness Skills among the Mentally Retarded Boys", Vyayam Vigyan, Vol. 40, No. 4,: 1-4.

Naveen K.V., Nagarathna R., Nagendra H.R., Telles S. (1997) "Yoga Breathing Through A Particular Nostril Increases Spatial Memory Scores Without Lateralized Effects", Psychological Reports Journal, 81(2):555-61.

Naveen K.V., Nagarathna R., Nagendra H.R., Telles S.,(1997)"Yoga Breathing Through A Particular Nostril Increases Spatial Memory Scores Without Lateralized Effects", Psychological Reports Journal, 81(2):555-61.

O. Preetha, (2006) "Effect of Selected Yogasanas and Aerobic Exercises on Selected Physical, Physiological and Psychological Variables in University Women Students", (Unpublished M. Phil Thesis) Pondicherry University, Pondicherry

Pailoor Subramanya and Shirley Tells, (2009) "Effect of Two Yoga-Based Relaxation Techniques on Memory Scores and State Anxiety", Bio Psycho Social Medicine, 3:8.

Pandya, Bhanuprasad A. (2014)Study the effect of yogasana on creativity and memory among the school children Ph.D. Thesis, M.S. University of Baroda, Vadodara.

Paqthani, prof. R.S. and Sah, Sapna (2015). "A qualitative investigation into how yoga can elevate learning capabilities in school –going children". International journal of advanced research in management. Vol. 6(3):152-156.

Pratap, V. (1968). Steadiness in normal before and after yogic practices, An exploratory study. Yoga Mimamsa Vol. XI 2, 1-13.

Raghav, Deepak (2018) Effects of selected yogic practices on height, eye vision and mental well being among school going children. Ph.D. Thesis, Aligarh Muslim University.

Rajmohan, C. (2001). *Effect of Yogasanas on memory, Attention, Achievement motivation and scholastic achievement of primary school children*. Unpublished Doctoral Dissertation. Alagappa University, Karaikudi.

Ray, U. S. et al. (2001)."Effects of yogic asanas and physical exercise on body flexibility in middle aged men". *Indian Journal of Physiology and Pharmacology*, Jan, 45(1):37-53.

Rejinadevi K. & Dr. C. Ramesh, (2017) "Effect of Yogic Practices on Selected Physiological Variables Among Basketball Players", International Journal of Computational Research and Development, Volume 2, Issue 2, Page Number 107-110.

Rocha, K., Ribeiro, A., Rocha, K., Sousa, M., Albuquerque, F., Ribeiro, S., & Silva, R. (2012).Improvement in physiological and psychological parameters after 6months of yoga practice. *Consciousness and cognition, 21*(2), 843-850.

Ross, Alyson M.S.N., R.N., and Thomas, Sue. F.A.A.N., Ph.D., R.N. (2010). "The Health Benefits of Yoga and Exercise" A Review of Comparison Studies". *The Journal of Alternative and Complementary Medicine.* Volume 16, pp. 3–12 Mary Ann Liebert, Inc.

Ryburn, W.M. (1956) Introduction to educational psychology, Oxford University Press,220.

Sandeep Berwal, & Savita Gahlawat (2013) "Effect of Yoga on Self-Concept and Emotional Maturity of Visually Challenged Students: An Experimental Study" Journal of the Indian Academy of Applied Psychology July 2013, Vol.39, No.2, 260-265.

Schell, F.J., Allolio B., Schonake O.W., (1994), "Physiological and Psychological effects of Hatha –Yoga exercise in healthy Women", International Journal of Psychosom. 41 (4) PP. 46-52

Sharma & Sharma, (2004): "A Study of Effect of Yogic Training on Attitude of Secondary School Level Boys", Vyayam Vigyan, 37:3 ,19.

Sharma, Sudhir Kumar, (2010) "Effects of Yogic Practices, Physical Exercises and Combination of Yogic Practices and Physical Exercises on Selected Motor Ability Components, Physiological and psychological Variables of Senior Secondary School Boys in Delhi", P E Y, 1.1, 28.

Singh, R (1996). A study on certain yogic asana and physical exercise on selected coordinative abilities unpublished. Ph.D. Thesis, Aligarh Muslim University.

Singh, R. (2010). "A study of certain yogic asanas and physical exercises on Balance ability". *Yoga Momamsa.* Vol. XLII No.1: 16-22.

Singh, R. (2010). "A study of certain yogic asanas and physical exercises on kinesthetic ability". *AMASS Multilateral Research Journal.*Vol.2, 8-12.

Singh, Samay (2007). Effect of Pranayama on selected physiological and psychological variables among school going children. Ph.D. Thesis, Major Dhyanchand Institute of Physical Education, Bundelkhand University, Jhansi (U.P.).

Steinhaus, Arthur H. (1966)., "Your Muscles See More than Your Eyes." Journal of Health Physical Education Recreation, 37:38,

Stephen Jeffrey Johnson (1974) Effects of Yoga - Therapy on Conflict Resolution, Self-concept, and Emotional Adjustment. Dissertation Abstracts International 34/10 p. 6385A.

Sukla, Deepti and Singh Joseph (2010) Yoga for Stress Relief. ICON Sports Abstract, International Conference hosted by IMS, GYM Banaras Hindu University, Varanasi.

Telles S, Singh N, Bhardwaj AK, Kumar A. & Balkrishna A. (2013) "Effect of yoga or physical exercise on physical, cognitive and emotional measures in children: a randomized controlled trial", Child Adolesc Psychiatry Ment Health. Nov 7;7(1):37.

Telles, S., S.K. Reddy and H.R. Nagendra, (2000) "Oxygen consumption and respiration. Following two yoga relaxation techniques". Appl. Psychophysiol. Biofeedback, 25:4, p.221-7.

Vinod et. al. (1984). Effect of Yogic Practices Performance on Adolescent Anxiety and Centcun Personality Trait: Yoga and Research International Conference Abstracts, Yoga Mimamsa 28 (29); 33-34.

Appendix - 3

Raw score of the HEIGHT of both the groups
(Control group, Experimental group)

S. no.	GROUPS			
	Control		Experimental	
	Pre	Post	Pre	Post
1.	171	172	152.6	153.2
2.	169.1	169.1	173.5	174.6
3.	159.1	159.1	158	158.9
4.	163.8	164	165.8	166.7
5.	177.8	177.8	175.9	176.8
6.	156.8	157.6	169.1	170.3
7.	157	158	154.5	155.6
8.	173.1	173.1	162.2	163.4
9.	177.1	177.1	175	176
10.	170.1	170.3	158	159
11.	158	158	162.4	163.6
12.	166.5	166.5	166.5	168.5
13.	163.4	163.6	163.8	165.8
14.	162.5	162.5	168	170
15.	153.5	153.5	170.5	170.9
16.	160.4	160.5	154.8	156
17.	178.9	179	161	162.1
18.	167	167.8	161.5	162
19.	169.8	170.1	176.1	177.2
20.	171.1	171.4	163.5	164.2
21.	168.5	168.5	170.8	171.9
22.	169.5	170	168	169
23.	160.4	161	175	177
24.	168.2	168.2	174	175.6
25.	173.1	173.1	170	171.3
26.	171	171	167	168.3
27.	173	173	163	164.2
28.	171.1	172	163.2	164.8
29.	168	168	169.4	170.8
30.	171.8	172	163.6	164.7

APPENDIX Raw score of the KINESTHETIC SENSE of both the groups (Control group, Experimental group)

S. no.	GROUPS			
	Control		*Experimental*	
	Pre	Post	Pre	Post
1.	4.67	3.67	5	1.67
2.	4	4	4.67	1
3.	3.67	3	5.67	2.33
4.	2.67	2.67	9	3
5.	7.67	6.67	4.67	4
6.	5.67	5.67	1.67	1
7.	5.67	5	5.3	2.33
8.	4.33	5	5	1.67
9.	5.67	4.67	5.3	0.66
10.	4.33	4	7.3	2
11.	3	3	3.67	1.33
12.	4.67	3.67	3.67	2.33
13.	2.33	3	8	2.67
14.	4	4	7	5
15.	6.67	7	3.67	3
16.	5	5	8.67	3
17.	5	5.67	11	5
18.	4.67	4.33	5.67	5
19.	3.67	4	18	3
20.	6	6.67	7.67	8
21.	8.33	8.67	14.33	4
22.	5	4	5.33	2
23.	11	11.67	9	8
24.	8	7.67	8.3	5.67
25.	12.3	11.67	4.33	1.67
26.	5.33	5	11.67	5
27.	5	6.67	5.67	3
28.	6.33	5.33	7.67	2
29.	7	6.67	10.67	4
30.	11	9	5.37	2

S. no.	GROUPS			
	Control		Experimental	
	Pre	Post	Pre	Post
1.	1	1	1	2
2.	1	1	1	2
3.	1	2	2	3
4.	2	2	1	2
5.	2	2	2	3
6.	1	1	2	3
7.	2	2	1	1
8.	1	1	1	2
9.	1	1	2	2
10.	1	1	1	1
11.	2	2	1	2
12.	2	2	1	2
13.	2	2	2	3
14.	1	1	1	2
15.	1	1	2	3
16.	2	2	2	2
17.	1	1	1	1
18.	1	1	1	2
19.	1	1	2	3
20.	2	2	1	2
21.	1	1	1	2
22.	1	1	1	2
23.	1	2	2	3
24.	2	2	1	2
25.	2	2	1	1
26.	1	1	2	2
27.	1	1	1	2
28.	2	2	2	2
29.	1	1	1	2
30.	2	2	1	1

APPENDIX Raw score of the MEMORY (repetition 2) of both the groups (Control group, Experimental group)

S. no.	GROUPS			
	Control		Experimental	
	Pre	Post	Pre	Post
1.	1	1	1	2
2.	2	2	1	2
3.	2	1	1	3
4.	2	3	1	1
5.	1	1	2	2
6.	2	2	1	3
7.	1	2	2	3
8.	1	1	2	3
9.	1	1	1	2
10.	2	2	2	3
11.	1	1	1	2
12.	1	1	1	2
13.	2	2	1	3
14.	1	1	1	2
15.	2	2	2	2
16.	1	1	1	2
17.	2	2	2	3
18.	1	1	1	2
19.	1	1	1	2
20.	2	2	1	2
21.	1	1	1	2
22.	1	1	1	2
23.	1	2	1	2
24.	1	1	2	3
25.	1	1	2	3
26.	2	2	2	3
27.	2	2	1	2
28.	1	2	1	3
29.	2	2	1	2
30.	2	2	2	3

APPENDIX Raw score of the MEMORY (repetition 3) of both the groups (Control group, Experimental group)

S. no.	GROUPS			
	Control		*Experimental*	
	Pre	Post	Pre	Post
1.	1	1	2	3
2.	2	3	2	3
3.	3	3	2	3
4.	3	3	1	2
5.	3	3	3	4
6.	2	2	3	4
7.	2	2	3	4
8.	2	2	2	3
9.	2	3	2	3
10.	2	3	2	3
11.	2	2	1	2
12.	3	3	2	3
13.	3	3	2	3
14.	1	2	2	3
15.	3	2	3	3
16.	2	3	3	3
17.	2	3	3	3
18.	2	2	1	2
19.	2	2	2	2
20.	3	3	2	3
21.	1	2	2	3
22.	2	2	1	2
23.	2	2	3	4
24.	2	2	2	3
25.	3	3	2	3
26.	2	2	3	3
27.	2	3	2	2
28.	2	2	2	3
29.	3	2	2	3
30.	3	3	2	3

 Raw score of the MEMORY (repetition 4) of both the groups (Control group, Experimental group)

S. no.	GROUPS			
	Control		*Experimental*	
	Pre	Post	Pre	Post
1.	2	2	3	3
2.	3	3	2	3
3.	4	4	3	4
4.	2	2	2	4
5.	2	2	2	4
6.	2	3	2	4
7.	3	3	4	4
8.	2	3	2	4
9.	3	3	2	3
10.	3	3	3	4
11.	2	2	2	3
12.	2	2	1	3
13.	2	2	3	3
14.	2	2	2	4
15.	4	4	2	4
16.	3	3	2	4
17.	2	2	4	4
18.	2	2	2	2
19.	3	3	3	4
20.	2	2	3	4
21.	2	2	2	3
22.	2	2	2	3
23.	3	3	2	4
24.	3	3	2	4
25.	2	2	3	4
26.	2	3	2	3
27.	3	3	1	3
28.	2	2	2	4
29.	4	4	3	4
30.	4	4	2	3

 Raw score of the CREATIVITY (The seeing problem test) of both the groups (Control group, Experimental group)

S. no.	GROUPS			
	Control		*Experimental*	
	Pre	Post	Pre	Post
1.	7	7	13	18
2.	18	18	15	23
3.	12	12	8	14
4.	14	15	14	21
5.	11	11	11	19
6.	6	6	14	19
7.	7	8	11	18
8.	11	11	16	20
9.	14	14	14	20
10.	5	6	5	13
11.	14	14	6	12
12.	15	16	10	18
13.	9	9	9	14
14.	9	9	14	19
15.	14	13	12	20
16.	12	12	6	13
17.	16	16	12	16
18.	6	6	14	22
19.	11	11	5	12
20.	16	16	14	21
21.	13	13	9	16
22.	4	4	11	20
23.	11	11	10	18
24.	14	14	14	19
25.	13	14	11	18
26.	12	12	11	15
27.	12	12	4	10
28.	12	12	13	17
29.	4	4	22	22
30.	9	9	16	18

APPENDIX **Raw score of the CREATIVITY (The unusual uses test) of both the groups (Control group, Experimental group)**

S. no.	GROUPS			
	Control		*Experimental*	
	Pre	Post	Pre	Post
1.	11	10	20	24
2.	22	21	39	42
3.	9	10	11	16
4.	16	17	15	19
5.	23	23	25	31
6.	8	10	17	22
7.	10	12	12	17
8.	26	27	24	28
9.	18	19	16	22
10.	10	12	4	9
11.	24	22	9	12
12.	32	30	36	39
13.	9	10	26	29
14.	24	22	21	28
15.	9	10	32	37
16.	22	23	29	32
17.	23	24	24	28
18.	7	9	32	35
19.	13	14	10	18
20.	47	40	29	31
21.	22	23	19	23
22.	8	10	21	24
23.	22	23	16	20
24.	32	31	32	36
25.	45	42	22	29
26.	9	10	8	14
27.	28	27	26	30
28.	40	35	34	36
29.	18	20	20	24
30.	33	35	47	45

APPENDIX **Raw score of the CREATIVITY (The consequence test) of both the groups (Control group, Experimental group)**

S. no.	GROUPS			
	Control		Experimental	
	Pre	Post	Pre	Post
1.	11	12	5	9
2.	13	14	16	21
3.	13	15	9	14
4.	11	10	9	14
5.	7	8	10	14
6.	7	9	6	8
7.	9	10	9	14
8.	5	7	8	12
9.	15	12	11	15
10.	6	7	5	11
11.	6	6	3	8
12.	12	10	7	13
13.	6	5	9	15
14.	6	8	18	26
15.	10	9	10	12
16.	10	11	6	14
17.	14	11	10	13
18.	2	5	8	12
19.	3	5	5	10
20.	7	8	15	18
21.	12	10	11	14
22.	11	9	8	13
23.	7	7	13	17
24.	12	11	12	17
25.	8	7	17	16
26.	6	6	20	23
27.	12	11	5	8
28.	10	9	7	9
29.	5	5	14	17
30.	10	10	7	11

 Raw score of the CREATIVITY (The test of inquisitiveness) of both the groups (Control group, Experimental group)

S. no.	GROUPS			
	Control		*Experimental*	
	Pre	Post	Pre	Post
1.	9	9	10	12
2.	11	11	12	15
3.	7	6	5	8
4.	9	9	9	12
5.	7	7	8	11
6.	10	10	9	10
7.	6	6	7	9
8.	5	5	9	13
9.	8	8	10	12
10.	10	10	6	10
11.	4	5	4	10
12.	13	12	10	16
13.	5	6	6	11
14.	10	9	8	14
15.	7	7	10	13
16.	12	13	4	9
17.	12	12	10	13
18.	6	7	13	17
19.	10	10	5	9
20.	16	15	8	11
21.	5	6	6	9
22.	13	14	10	12
23.	4	5	12	17
24.	11	11	11	19
25.	8	9	15	21
26.	5	6	11	17
27.	6	6	6	9
28.	12	12	5	7
29.	6	7	16	19
30.	6	6	10	16

S. no.	Control		Experimental	
	Pre	Post	Pre	Post
1.	10	10	19	23
2.	20	21	10	12
3.	26	26	20	22
4.	13	14	25	28
5.	24	25	36	39
6.	27	26	25	28
7.	17	15	8	9
8.	11	13	29	25
9.	24	23	27	31
10.	29	27	11	15
11.	21	22	15	18
12.	17	18	8	12
13.	30	31	15	17
14.	20	22	17	21
15.	33	30	30	33
16.	23	23	19	24
17.	21	21	17	21
18.	10	11	15	17
19.	28	26	18	21
20.	13	14	23	27
21.	10	13	17	19
22.	24	24	16	19
23.	12	13	30	32
24.	16	17	22	27
25.	15	17	18	22
26.	19	18	34	37
27.	11	13	8	11
28.	18	18	11	15
29.	34	33	25	26
30.	11	13	10	12

APPENDIX **Raw score of the CREATIVITY (The blocks test of creativity) of both the groups (Control group, Experimental group)**

S. no.	GROUPS			
	Control		*Experimental*	
	Pre	Post	Pre	Post
1.	40	44	13	17
2.	68	67	42	45
3.	29	30	35	36
4.	15	17	14	18
5.	33	34	34	36
6.	31	33	57	60
7.	15	18	40	44
8.	28	27	49	51
9.	34	33	25	29
10.	20	21	28	32
11.	47	48	31	33
12.	39	37	39	42
13.	28	28	33	37
14.	25	27	37	39
15.	37	31	15	19
16.	25	29	13	15
17.	50	45	55	57
18.	21	28	21	28
19.	38	37	39	40
20.	42	43	47	51
21.	28	27	31	39
22.	55	51	25	29
23.	42	44	25	27
24.	35	37	23	25
25.	33	35	56	59
26.	53	55	39	43
27.	42	44	42	48
28.	37	39	28	32
29.	39	36	68	67
30.	13	18	25	28

Appendix – 4

Description of Yogic Practices

Surya Namaskar

Method

Asana 1: Pranamasana (Prayer Pose)

Bring your hands closer to join both of your palms. Place the hands on the center of your chest. This position is known as Namaskar Mudra. Breathe normally and relax the whole body.

Asana 2: Hastauttanasana (Raised Arms Pose)

With an inhalation raise your arms and head upwards. Slowly and gently bend your torso backward, moving your arms and head backward too. Bend only as far as you feel comfortable. Feel the chest expanding and your abdomen stretching while staying in the pose

Asana 3: Padahastasana (Hand to foot pose)

Inhale as you bend forward using your hip muscles. Keep the arms by the side of your ears. Bend until your palms or fingers touch the floor. Keep the knees straight. Try to touch your knees with your forehead. Feel the stretch of the spine as you bend forward.

Asana 4: Ashwa Sanchalanasana (Equestrian Pose)

Slightly bend your knees to place the palms on the floor, parallel to your feet. As you inhale, take the right foot back as far as you can, resting its big toes on the floor. Gently keep the right knee on the ground, avoid pressing it against the floor. The left knee remains bent. Expand the chest and look upwards. Keep the palms or fingers on the floor.

Asana 5: Adho MukhaSavasana or Parvatasana (Downward Facing Dog)

With an exhalation move the front leg back to place it beside the right leg. Move your hips upwards, sucking in your belly. Move the head towards the floor and look at your navel. Try to keep the heels on the floor. The arms and legs must be straight.

Distribute the body weight equally on arms and legs. Be aware of the stretching of shoulders and back of the legs.

Asana 6: Ashtanga Namanasana (Salute with eight parts)

From Adho Mukha Savasana, gently put your knees on the floor. Place your chest right between both of your hands. Rest the chin on the floor. The buttocks and abdomen remain lifted. In this asana, eight parts of the body touch the ground, saluting the sun. Chin, chest, both hands, knees and big toes. That's why it is known as 'salute with eight parts'.

Asana 7: Bhujangasana (Cobra Pose)

As you inhale move the body forward to come into Bhujangasana. Arch the back backward as much as you can. The arms must be straight or slightly bent in the final position. Move the head backward and gaze upwards.

Asana 8: Adho Mukha Savasana or Parvatasana (Downward Facing Dog)

Use the strength of your arms to lift the buttocks upwards to move into Parvatasana.

Asana 9: Ashwa Sanchalanasana (Equestrian Pose)

The hands and feet remain in the same position. Move the left leg and place it right between the hands.

Asana 10: Padahastasana (Hand to foot pose)

Keep the front leg in the same position. With an exhalation, lift the right leg placing the right foot beside the left foot. Straighten the legs, keep the hands by the side of the feet. Try to bring the forehead close to the knees.

Asana 11: Hastauttanasana (Raised Arms Pose)

As you inhale, raise the body while keeping the arms straight and close to the ears. Stretch upwards and then backward. Keep the knees straight.

Asana 12: Pranamasana (Prayer Pose)

Straighten the trunk, arms and head. Exhale and simply lower the arms in Namaskar mudra. Relax the whole body.

All the 12 poses are repeated again with a slight change of leg position in asana 4th and 9th. That's what makes one round of Surya Namaskar. When you practice again, the left foot goes back in 4th asana instead of right foot this time. In the 9th asana, the right foot comes in front instead of left. So it takes 24 poses in total to complete one round of Surya Namaskar.

Ardhachandrasana

Method

- Stand straight on the ground, and take a gap between your feet.

- With deeply breathing (inhale), raise your one arm,say the right .

- Bend to the left side(exhale).

- Left hand go down on the left side (near knee)

- Try to maintain this pose as long as you can and come back slowly to the starting position

- And repeat same for the other side

Vrikshasasana

Method

- Stand with the feet together, focus the gaze on a fixed point at eye level.

- Bending the right knee place the foot on the left thigh in the half Lotus position and stand steadily like a tree.

- Place the both palm of the hands together in front of the chest in Pranam Mudra.

- This is the starting position. Sift the weight to the left leg bend the left knee and slowly lower the body maintaining balance until the right knee rests on the floor.

- Hold the final position for a short duration with the weight evenly balanced on the left foot and right knee, slowly rise the body by strengthening the left knee, and return to the starting position.

- Released the right leg and lower into the floor; the practice can be repeated on the other side.

Tadasana

Method

- Stand straight on the ground, and take a small gap between your feet.

- with deeply breathing (inhale), raise your both arms.

- Keep your arms upward by interlocking your fingers.

- Now come on the toes by raising your heels simultaneously

- Feel the pressure of stretching from toes to fingers.

- Try to maintain this pose as long as you can with slow and deep breathing.

- Now come to the original position with deep breathing (exhale).

- You can perform the number of rounds as per your convenience after having relaxation for a while.

Supt Vajrasana

Method

- Sit comfortably in Vajrasana.

- Keeping your palms on the floor beside the buttocks, your fingers pointing to the front.

- Slowly bend back, putting the proper forearm and also the elbow on the bottom so the left.

- Slowly bring down your head to the ground while arching the back. Place your hands on the thighs.

- Try to stay the lower legs connected with the ground. If necessary, separate the knees.

- Make certain that you simply don't seem to be overstraining the muscles and ligaments of the legs.

- Close the eyes and relax the body.

- Breathe deeply and slowly within the final position.

- Release within the reverse order, inhaling and taking the support of the elbows and also the arms raise the top higher than the bottom.

- Then shift the weight on the left arm and elbow by slippery the body, then slowly returning to the beginning position.

- Never leave the ultimate position by straightening the legs first; it's going to dislocate the knee joints.

- Repeat this process for for specific time determined by the researcher.

Vakrasana

Method

- Sit up with the legs stretched out straight in front of you on the floor.

- Then raises one of his knees, say the right, and withdraws his foot till it rests by the side of his left knee.

- Next places his right hand behind his back without much twisting his trunk.

- Thereafter the left arm passed round the right knee from outside and the left palm is placed on the ground.

- In doing this the student pushes the right knee as far to the left as possible, all the while trying to twist his trunk to the right as best as he can.

- The knee is, however, kept firmly in its position, offering good resistance to the opposite arm.

- The last part of the technique is gone through when the student turns his face to the right, till his chin finds itself coming exactly over the right shoulder. This secures the complete twist to the right for the spinal column.

Paschimottanasana

Method

- Sit up with the legs stretched out straight in front of you on the floor.

- Keep the spine erect and toes flexed towards you.

- Bring your respiration to normal.

- Breathing in, slowly raise your both the arms straight above your head and stretch up.

- Slowly breathe out and bend forward from the hip joint, chin moving toward the toes keeping the spine erect.

- Place your hands on your legs, wherever they reach, without putting much effort.

- If possible hold of your toes and pull on them to help you go forward.

- Stay in this position as long as possible.

- After the exertion limit reached inhale and raise up stretching up your arms straight above your head.

- Breathe out and bring your arms down placing the palms on the ground.

- Relax for a while and try to feel the changes occurred in the body.

Dhanurasana

Method

- Lie on your stomach

- Hold your both feet with your hands making a back bend and positioning like a bow.

- Pull your both feet slowly – slowly, as much as you can.

- Look straight ahead with a smile in your face.

- Keep the pose stable while paying attention to your breath.

- After 1-20 seconds as you exhale, gently bring your legs and chest to the ground and relax.

Sarvangasana

Method

- Lie supine on the mat, feet together.

- Arms by the side of the thighs with palms downwards.

- Gracefully raise the legs together without bending the knees till it from 45^0 to the ground. Raise the legs further to 90^0 positions.

- Now gradually raise the buttocks and trunk and take the legs behind the head. Resting elbow on the ground firmly, support the back with palms, try to make the back and the legs straight, perpendicular to the ground.

- Stretch the tows upward.

- There should be proper chin lock. Relaxingly, support the body on the shoulder with normal breathing.

- Maintain the position for specific time determined by the researcher and then slowly release the posture.

Halasana

Method

- Lie flat on the back, feet together arms by the side with palms downwards.

- Keeping the whole of the spine pressed to the floor; slowly raise the legs with feet together up to 90^0 and pause for three or four respiration.

- Now gradually raise the buttocks and trunk as well as without lifting the head so that the toes touch the ground behind the head.

- Stretch out your legs and allow your toes to move on the ground as far as possible from your head.

- Do not strain. If your toes do not touch the floor, do not worry, within few practice, toes will reach the floor. Maintain the position for specific time determined by the researcher and then slowly release the posture.

Chakrasana

Method

- Lie down on your back with feet apart, bend your knees and place your feet on the ground close to your body.

- Now bring your palms under your shoulders such that the fingers point towards the shoulders and the elbows are shoulder width apart.

- Inhale and press your palms firmly into the floor.

- Lift your shoulders and elbow firmly into the floor

- Your Feet should be pressed firmly into the floor.

- Inhale and lift your hips up.

- The spine should be rolled up so that it may seem to resemble a semi circular arch or wheel.

- Straighten out your arms and legs as much as possible so that the hips and chest maybe

- Pushed up.

- Hold this pose for at least 15-30 seconds.

- To go back to original, bend your elbows to lower your head and shoulders to the floor.

- Then bend your knees and bring your spine and hips back to the ground and relax.

Kapalbhati

Method

- First, sit on the Padmasana and close your eyes and keep the spine straight.

- Now take a deep breath (inhale deeply) through your both nostrils until your lungs are full with air.

- Now Exhale through both nostrils forcefully, so your stomach will go deep inside. As you exhale you feel some pressure in your stomach.

- While the process of exhaling there is a hissing sound, at this point try to think that your disorders are coming out of your nose.

- Repeat this process for specific time determined by the researcher

AnulomVilom

Method

- Anulom Vilom Pranayama is very easy to do, first of all close your eyes and sit in Padmasana and rest your hands on your knees.

- Close the right nostril with the right thumb. Inhale slowly through the left nostril, inhale the oxygen as much as you can, this will fill your lungs with air.

- Remove your thumb from your right nostril and close your left nostrilwith your fingers exhale air from right nostril.

- When you exhale after that inhale with your right nostril and exhale from left nostril.

- Close left nostril with the help of left hand fingers and right nostril from the right hand thumb.

- Be focused and concentrate on your breathing and repeat same process for specific time determined by the researcher

Bhramari

Method

- Sit on the Padmasana or any other sitting Asana.

- Close your eyes and breathe deeply.

- Now close your ears lids or flaps with your thumbs.

- Place your index finger just above your eyebrows and the rest of your Fingers over your eyes with your middle fingers.

- Applying very gentle pressure to the sides of your nose.

- Now concentrate your mind on the area between your eyebrows.

- Keep your mouth closed; breathe out slowly through your nose with making a humming sound of Om.

- Repeat this process for specific time determined by the researcher. Important thing is that while doing this Pranayama assumes that you are being connected to all the positive energies of the universe.

Yoga Nidra

Method

- Lie down straight on your back in Corpse Pose (Shavasana). Close your eyes and relax. Take a few deep breaths in and out. Remember to take slow and relaxed breaths.

- Start by gently taking your attention to your right foot. Keep your attention there for a few seconds, while relaxing your foot. Then gently move your attention up to the right knee, right thigh and hip. Become aware of your whole right leg.

- Gently, repeat this process for the left leg.

- Take your attention to all parts of the body: genital area, stomach, navel region and chest.

- Take your attention to the right shoulder, right arm, palms, and fingers. Repeat this on the left shoulder, left arm, throat, face, and finally the top of the head.

- Take a deep breath in and observe the sensations in your body. Relax in this state for a few minutes.

- Slowly becoming aware of your body and surroundings, turn to your right side and keep lying down for a few more minutes. Rolling over to the right side makes the breath flow through the left nostril which helps cool the body.

- Taking your own time, you may then slowly sit up, and whenever you feel comfortable, slowly and gradually open your eyes.

Shavasana

Method

- Lie flat on the back with the arms about 15 cm away from the body, palms facing upward.

- Let the fingers curl up slightly.

- Move the feet slightly apart to a comfortable position and close the eyes. The head and spine should be in a straight line.

- Make sure the head does not fall to one side or the other.

- Relax the whole body and stop all physical movement.

- Become aware of the natural breath and allow it to become rhythmic and relaxed.

- If the mind can be kept on the breath for a few minutes the body will relax.

Makarasana

Method

- Lie flat on the stomach.

- Raise the head and shoulders and rest the chin in the palms of

- The hands with the elbows on the floor.

- Keep the elbows together for a more pronounced arch to the spine. Separate the elbows slightly to relieve excess pressure on the neck.

- In Makrasana the effect is felt at two points: the neck and the lower back.

- If the elbows are too far in front, tension will be felt in the neck; if they are drawn too

- Close to the chest, tension will be felt more in the lower back. Adjust the position of

- The elbows so that these two points are equally balanced.

- The ideal position is when the whole spine is equally relaxed. Relax the whole body and closes the eyes.